# HOME REPAIR AND IMPROVEMENT

# WINDOWS AND DOORS

TIME®
LIFE
BOOKS

OTHER PUBLICATIONS:

Do It Yourself
The Time-Life Complete Gardener
Home Repair and Improvement
The Art of Woodworking
Fix It Yourself

Cooking
Weight Watchers® Smart Choice Recipe Collection
Great Taste/Low Fat
Williams-Sonoma Kitchen Library

History
The American Story
Voices of the Civil War
The American Indians
Lost Civilizations
Mysteries of the Unknown
Time Frame
The Civil War
Cultural Atlas

Time-Life Kids
Family Time Bible Stories
Library of First Questions and Answers
A Child's First Library of Learning
I Love Math
Nature Company Discoveries
Understanding Science & Nature

Science/Nature
Voyage Through the Universe

For information on and a full description
of any of the Time-Life Books series listed above,
please call 1-800-621-7026 or write:

Reader Information
Time-Life Customer Service
P.O. Box C-32068
Richmond Virginia 23261-2068

HOME REPAIR AND IMPROVEMENT

# WINDOWS AND DOORS

BY THE EDITORS OF TIME-LIFE BOOKS, ALEXANDRIA, VIRGINIA

*The Consultants*
Jeff Palumbo is a registered journeyman
carpenter who has a home-building and
remodeling business in northern Virginia.
His interest in carpentry was sparked
by his grandfather, a master carpenter
with more than 50 years' experience.
Mr. Palumbo teaches in the Fairfax County
Adult Education Program.

Mark M. Steele is a professional home
inspector in the Washington, D.C., area.
He has developed and conducted training
programs in home-ownership skills for first-
time homeowners. He appears frequently
on televison and radio as an expert in home
repair and consumer topics.

# CONTENTS

# Curing the Common Ailments

It's not surprising that doors and windows require frequent maintenance; they are opened and closed countless times a year and often deal with the worst punishment the elements can dish out. The most common repairs, such as replacing a broken sash cord, are easy fixes, once you know how to get at the problem. More serious ailments can be cured with a variety of time-proven techniques.

Plugging screw holes to tighten hinges →

# The Four Basic Types of Windows

**B**efore attempting any repairs, examine your window to see how it operates. Shown below and on the following page are four common types of movable windows: double-hung, casement, awning, and sliding. All of them have the same basic parts: glazed sashes, a frame, and narrow strips at the sides and top of the frame to hold the sash in place.

The difference between them is how they open: Double-hung windows slide up and down, casement and awning windows swing outward, and sliding windows are pushed from side to side. Each type of window has a different mechanism and a few special parts.

Although the windows shown here are traditional wood windows, models made of other materials, such as vinyl or aluminum, are also available in the four basic types.

On the opposite page you will find a glossary that includes window terms commonly used in finish carpentry. Many of these words, such as jamb, rail, and stop, also apply to doors, while some terms are particular to each.

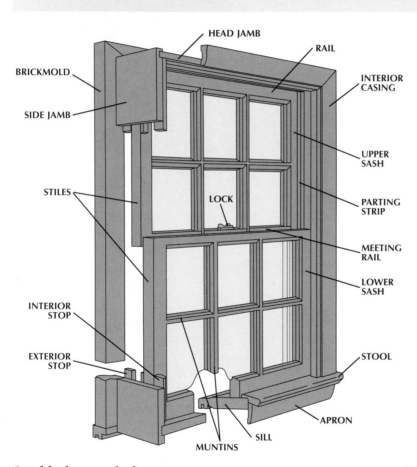

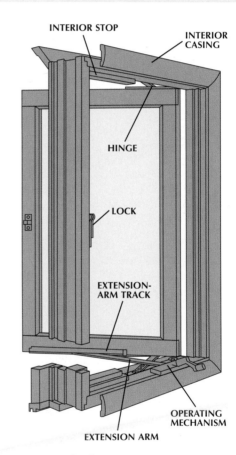

## Double-hung windows.

The frame consists of two side jambs; a head, or top, jamb; and a two-piece bottom made of a sill outside and a stool inside, trimmed with an apron. Sliding inside the jambs are a lower and an upper sash. (In a single-hung window only the lower, or inner, sash moves.) The sashes are held by three thin pieces: a blind stop on the outside, a parting strip between the sashes, and an interior stop. Each sash has two horizontal rails and two vertical stiles. Many sashes are divided by muntins, which may secure separate panes of glass or simply be glued to the outside of a single pane. The joints between the jambs and the wall indoors are hidden by three pieces of interior casing; the joints between the jambs and the exterior siding are covered by exterior casing, called brickmold.

## Casement windows.

These sashes, hung singly or in pairs, have hinges mounted to top and bottom rails; because the sashes swing outward there are no exterior stops. In most modern casement windows, the sash is moved by an operating mechanism—a geared crank and an extension arm that slides in a track on the lower rail; in many older windows, the sash is pushed or pulled by hand or by a hand-held rod. The latch and lock are mounted on the stile and side jamb opposite the hinges. Casement windows often have no stool or apron; instead, a bottom stop, and a fourth piece of interior casing complete the frame.

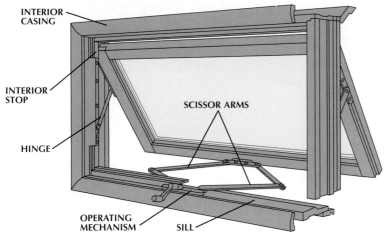

INTERIOR CASING

INTERIOR STOP

HINGE

SCISSOR ARMS

OPERATING MECHANISM

SILL

## Awning windows.

The sash, hinged near the top of each stile, swings out at the bottom, ventilating a room while blocking rain. In this widely used design, the sash is moved by an operating mechanism with two scissor arms that fold against the sill when the window is closed. Like a casement window, the awning window often has interior casing on the bottom instead of an apron and stool.

A hopper window, which swings out at the top, is virtually identical in construction to an awning window.

## Sliding windows.

Sashes slide horizontally, generally on plastic rollers. These run along the channels of metal or vinyl jamb liners at the top and bottom of the window frame. A latch and lock are mounted on the meeting stiles. In most models, the sashes can be removed without dismantling the window frame—you simply lift them up and tilt the bottom rail out of its channel. The bottom of the window is typically trimmed with casing rather than with an apron and stool.

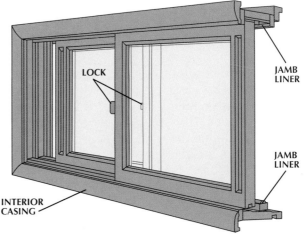

LOCK

JAMB LINER

JAMB LINER

INTERIOR CASING

## THE LANGUAGE OF WINDOWS AND DOORS

**Apron:** The inside trim that lies flat against the wall beneath the stool (the interior window sill). It covers the gap between the stool and the wall.

**Brickmold:** The trim around the outside of a door or window.

**Casing:** The interior trim around the top and sides of a window or door.

**Dado:** A rectangular groove in a board, designed to accept the edge of a second piece.

**Finish frame:** The stationary pieces immediately adjacent to the movable parts of a window or door.

**Jamb:** A piece at the side or top of the finish frame around a window or door The top piece is called the head jamb; the term jamb used alone usually refers to the side pieces.

**Light:** A window, a section of a divided window, or a pane set in a window.

**Miter:** An angle cut into an edge to fit a matching angle in another piece; many trim ends are cut at 45° angles to form a right-angle joint.

**Mortise:** A recess cut in a piece of wood. Typically fitted with hardware, such as a hinge.

**Mullion:** A slender vertical bar separating adjoining windows; sometimes also used to refer to a muntin.

**Muntin:** A narrow vertical or horizontal strip separating the panes of a window.

**Parting strip:** A narrow piece of molding along the inner top and sides of the frame of a double-hung window, separating the upper and lower sashes.

**Rabbet:** A step cut in the edge of a board to form a joint with another board.

**Rail:** The horizontal top or bottom piece of a door or a window sash.

**Rough frame:** The framework, usually of heavy boards, surrounding a door or window opening and covered by trim.

**Sash:** The movable part of any window, or the frame that holds the glass.

**Sill:** The exterior horizontal piece at the bottom of a window frame, generally slanted down to shed water. The inside piece, commonly mislabeled the sill, is properly called the stool.

**Stile:** A vertical side piece of a door or a window sash.

**Stool:** The horizontal piece of inside trim at the base of a window, resting on the sill and projecting into the room.

**Stop:** A strip of trim along the face of a door or window jamb, which prevents a door or a casement window from swinging too far and creates channels for double-hung window sashes.

**Threshold:** A strip fastened to the floor beneath a door.

# Why Windows Stick—and How to Free Them

The sashes of double-hung windows are sometimes difficult to operate. Many times, the repair is as simple as easing the sash channels; or you may need to replace part or all of the mechanism.

**Binding Sashes:** The most common cause of a sticking sash is a layer of paint and dirt that narrows the channels between the stops. This layer can be removed as explained opposite.

If the channels are clean, check the jamb with a straightedge to see whether the sash is bowed; slip a piece of paper along the joints between the stops and the sash to find where it is binding. You may be able to free it by forcing the jamb or stop away from it slightly *(opposite)*.

Sometimes the sash can be freed by removing the stop *(page 28)*, moving it back slightly, and renailing it to the jamb—but be sure to move

it only a fraction of an inch or the sash will rattle. Never try to plane down the sides of a sash—no matter how little wood you remove, you will almost certainly end up with a rattling sash.

**Frozen Sashes:** A sash that will not budge at all may be painted shut and have to be pried open *(page 12)* or it may be nailed shut. To remove finishing nails, drive them completely through the sash with a pin punch; pull any large-headed nails with carpenter's nippers *(page 29)*; then try to free the sash by the techniques described on page 12.

**Faulty Mechanisms:** If the channel is clean and the jamb straight but the sash jams partway open, or if it falls when the window is opened, the mechanism is probably at fault and can be repaired or replaced.

Older double-hung windows are counterbalanced by a pulley and a cord with a weight. A broken cord can be replaced *(pages 13-14)*; do not use ordinary rope, which wears out too quickly.

Newer double-hung windows use a variety of mechanisms. Wood windows may have window channels *(page 15)*, or tape or cord balances *(pages 17-18)*; vinyl and aluminum windows normally rely on block-and-tackle balances *(page 18)*; while tube balances are used on all types of windows *(page 16)*.

If the balance on one side of a window breaks, it is a good idea to replace both. Take one of the old balances with you to the supplier to get the right type. In some cases you will need to know the weight of the sash—a balance that is not suitable for your window can be dangerous, allowing the sash to drop suddenly.

 **TOOLS**

Wood chisel
Mallet
Hammer
Pin punch
Screwdriver
Wide-blade putty knife

Utility knife
Shears
Pry bar
Carpenter's nippers
Pliers
Long-nose pliers
Diagonal-cutting pliers
Electric drill

 **MATERIALS**

Steel wool
Sandpaper (medium grade)
Paraffin block
Silicone spray lubricant

Galvanized nails ($1\frac{1}{2}$")
Galvanized wood screws ($\frac{3}{4}$"
    No. 6, $\frac{1}{2}$" No. 8, $2\frac{1}{2}$" No. 12)
Replacement nails and screws
Sash cord or chain
Wire

 **SAFETY TIPS**

*Wear goggles to protect your eyes from flying debris when scraping or prying.*

 **CAUTION**

## Working Safely with Lead

*The paint used in homes built or remodeled before 1978 may contain lead. Scraping or sanding this paint can release particles into the air, posing a health risk. To find out if your paint contains lead, use a home test kit available in hardware stores, or contact your local health department or environmental protection office for other testing options. If you suspect that the paint you are removing may contain lead, keep children, pets, and pregnant women away from the work area.*

*Cover the floors, then spray the paint with water before scraping it to keep dust down. Wear gloves and a high-efficiency particulate (HEPA) respirator while working, and set up a fan to blow the dust outside. When you are finished, mop the area twice and carefully sweep up any debris with a vacuum cleaner outfitted with an HEPA filter. Shower and wash hair, and launder clothing separately.*

# EASING A TIGHT SASH

## Cleaning the channels.

◆ On wooden or metal channels, run a chisel, flat side out, along the surfaces touched by the sash. Work on the jambs first, then the sides of the stops and the parting strips, if any. If necessary, remove the sash *(page 13)* to do a thorough job. Weather stripping and plastic channels should be cleaned with steel wool since a chisel might damage the surfaces.

◆ Sand wood channels and paint them if you wish. Do not sand or paint metal or plastic channels.

◆ Lubricate wood jambs, stops, and parting strips by running a block of household paraffin up and down the channels three or four times. For metal and plastic jambs apply silicone spray, which is also suitable for wood.

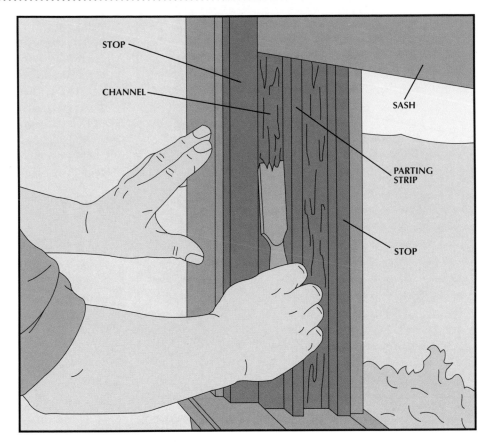

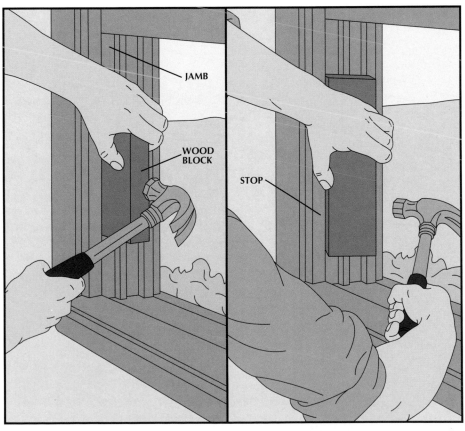

## Straightening bowed jambs and stops.

◆ Set a wood block about 6 inches long against the back of the channel at the point where the sash sticks, and strike the block no more than five or six times with a hammer *(far left)*.

◆ If this treatment makes the sash slide more easily, drive $2\frac{1}{2}$-inch galvanized No. 12 flat-head screws about 3 inches apart through the jamb and into the jack stud behind it to straighten the jamb. If hammering the jamb does not make the sash slide more easily, do not repeat the procedure—continued pounding could damage the window frame. Instead, remove the sashes *(pages 13-15)* and straighten the jamb as you would for a door *(pages 25)*.

If a sash binds against a stop, set the block against the side of the stop and tap it with a hammer several times *(near left)*; do not drive screws into the stop.

# FREEING A FROZEN SASH

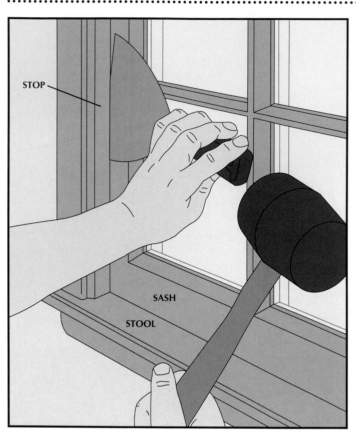

**Breaking a paint seal.**
◆ Force a wide-blade putty knife or a window zipper *(photograph)* into the joint between the sash and the stop. Work the tool around both sides of the sash, then force it into the joint between the sash and the stool.
◆ If the sash still refuses to move, go outside the house and check the joint between the sash and the parting strip; repeat the procedure there if necessary.

**Prying open a double-hung window.**
◆ Force the blade of a heavy screwdriver between the sash and the jamb; if the sash has a groove for a sash cord, use it as the point of entry for the blade *(right)*.
◆ Pry the sash away from the jamb, then repeat the procedure at the other side of the sash. Continue to work the sash to the right and left until you can slide it open.

**Prying the sash up from outside.**
◆ If the window remains stuck, go outside the house and wedge a pry bar between the finish sill and the sash.
◆ Set a block of wood on the sill under the pry bar for leverage and, working first under the corners of the sash, pry the sash up.

# REPLACING A BROKEN SASH CORD

## 1. Removing the lower sash.

The lower sash cord is generally the first to break; if the upper cord is broken, see page 15. In either case, replace the cord on the opposite side of the sash at the same time.

◆ Pry off the stop *(page 28)* on the side of the window with the broken cord. Raise the sash slightly, angle it toward you, and pull it sideways to free the other side of its stop *(right)*.

◆ Pull the knot at the sash end of the broken cord down with a pair of long-nose pliers and set the piece of cord aside.

◆ On the other side of the sash, pull the cord out of the sash. Tie a larger knot in the end of the cord and guide the knot up to rest against the pulley.

◆ Remove any weather stripping from the lower part of the jamb.

◆ If your window has interlocking metal weather stripping, which fits into a groove in the sash, remove the stop from the other side of the window and have a helper raise the sash and hold it at the top of the window frame.

◆ Using carpenter's nippers, remove the nails that fasten the weather stripping to the frame; then carefully angle both the weather stripping and the sash out of the window frame.

UPPER SASH

PULLEY

LOWER SASH

STOP

SASH WEIGHT

CASING

ACCESS PLATE

PARTING STRIP

## 2. Taking out the access plate.

If your window does not have an access plate, you will have to remove the casing *(page 29)* to get at the sash weight.

◆ Remove the screws at the top and bottom of the access plate and pry the plate out of the jamb with an old chisel *(left)*. If the parting strip covers one edge of the access plate, remove the strip *(page 15)* before prying out the plate. For an access plate that is concealed by paint, rap on the lower part of the sash channel with a hammer. When the outline of the plate appears, cut around it with a utility knife, then remove the screws and pry out the plate.

◆ Reach into the access hole, take out the sash weight, and untie the broken cord. Add 1 foot to the total length of the broken cord and cut a new cord with shears or a utility knife to this length. If you are using a chain, cut it with diagonal-cutting pliers.

### 3. Putting in the new cord.

◆ Tie one end of a length of string to a bent nail and the other end to the new sash cord. Feed the nail over the pulley into the access hole; then pull the cord over the pulley and down to the access hole *(left)*.
◆ Untie the string and tie the cord to the sash weight, leaving about 3 inches of surplus cord.
◆ Rest the sash on the sill and refasten the undamaged cord on the opposite side.

If you are using a sash chain, put a nail through a link at one end to keep the chain from slipping through the pulley and feed the other end over the pulley until it appears at the access hole. Put the end of the chain through the eye of the weight and fasten the loop with thin wire or with clips provided by the manufacturer.

### 4. Attaching the new cord to the sash.

◆ With the sash resting on the sill, pull down on the new cord until the sash weight touches the pulley, then lower the weight about 2 inches.
◆ Thread the cord into its groove in the sash. Tie a knot in the cord at the level of the hole in the side of the sash, cut off any extra cord, and insert the knot in the hole.
◆ Hold the sash in its track and slide it all the way up; the bottom of the weight should be visible in the access hole, about 2 inches above the bottom of the window frame. If necessary, adjust the cord by retying it at the sash weight.
◆ Replace the access plate, any weather stripping, and the stop; use short nails or screws that will not obstruct the sash weight.

To attach a sash chain, thread the chain into the groove in the sash and drive $\frac{3}{4}$-inch No. 6 wood screws through two of its links into the sash *(inset)*.

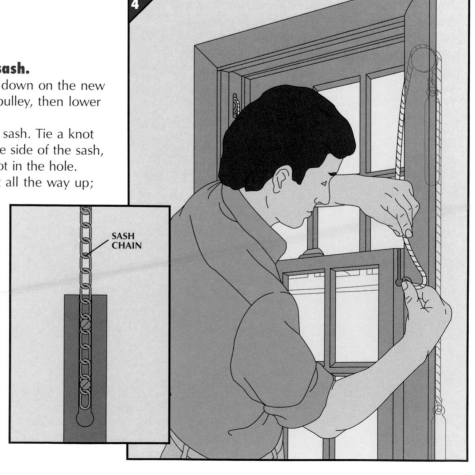

# FIXING THE UPPER SASH CORD

## Removing the upper sash

◆ After removing a side stop and the lower sash *(page 13)*, lower the upper sash.

◆ Drill a pilot hole in the parting strip about 3 inches from the top and thread a short wood screw into it. Caution: Do not drive the screw clear through the strip into the jamb.

◆ Pull steadily on the screw with a pair of pliers until you can slip a chisel behind the end of the

parting strip. From this point, pry the strip out a little at a time with the chisel, moving the tool downward as the gap widens between the jamb and the parting strip.

◆ When the top half of the strip is free, slide the sash to the top of the window frame, then pry out the lower half of the parting strip.

◆ Follow the procedures outlined in Steps 2 to 4 on pages 13 and 14 to replace the sash cord.

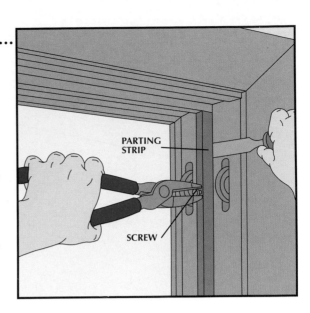

# NEW WINDOW CHANNELS

## 1. Removing the channels.

Window channels rely on tracks with tabs and springs hidden behind the track to hold the sashes up.

◆ With carpenter's nippers, pull the nails or staples that fasten the channels to the side jambs. Remove any interior stops from the side and head jambs *(page 28)* and slide both sashes to the middle of the window.

◆ Working at one channel while a helper works at the other, tilt the tops of both channels inward *(left)*. Let the bottoms slide partway outdoors from the window, and remove both the channels and sashes as a single unit.

◆ Set the bottoms of the channels on the floor and, while your helper holds them upright against the sashes, slide the sashes up and out of the channels.

## 2. Installing new channels.

◆ Have your helper hold the new channels upright on the floor, with the angles cut by the manufacturer at their bottoms matching the slant of the window's finish sill. Slide the bottom sash into the channel tracks, then the upper sash *(right)*.

◆ Together, lift the entire unit into the window frame, tilting it as described in Step 1 *(above)*.

◆ Position the channels against the blind stops and fasten them to the side jambs with $1\frac{1}{2}$-inch galvanized nails or No. 8 wood screws at the top and bottom of each track. Replace the interior stops.

# INSTALLING TUBE BALANCES

TUBE

MOUNTING BRACKET

## 1. Removing a balance.

Inside each cylindrical tube balance, a spring-loaded spiral rod holds the sash up. Turning the rod as shown below adjusts the tension on the spring *(Step 2)*, and this alone may free a sticky sash. If this fails, you will need to remove and replace the balance.

◆ Starting on one side of the window, remove both the stop *(page 28)* and the screw that fastens the top of the tube to the side jamb *(left)*.

◆ Raise the sash a foot or so, angle the side of the sash inward out of the window frame, and support the sash on wooden blocks.

◆ If the spiral rod inside the tube is fastened to the mounting bracket on the bottom edge of the sash with a detachable hook, unhook it; otherwise, unscrew the bracket. Remove the tube from its groove.

If your tube balances are built into channels *(page 15, Step 1)*, remove the channels and sashes together.

## 2. Installing a new balance.

◆ Set the new tube into the groove and screw the top of it to the side jamb.

◆ Pull the spiral rod down until it is fully extended, then tighten the spring inside by turning the rod clockwise about four complete revolutions.

◆ Let the rod retract into the tube until you can screw the mounting bracket to the bottom of the sash.

◆ Repeat steps 1 and 2 to replace the balance on the other side. Make sure that the rod is tightened the same number of times on both sides.

◆ Slide the sash up and down. If it creeps up when you release it, loosen both balance springs by turning the rods counterclockwise; if it moves down, turn the rods clockwise to tighten the spring. When the balance is correct, replace the stops.

SPIRAL ROD

# CHANGING TAPE BALANCES

TAPE BALANCE DRUM FOR UPPER SASH

LOWER SASH DRUM

TAPE

## Replacing the drums.

Tape balances are spring-loaded drums fitted into pockets on each side of the window frame. Thin metal tapes unreel from the drums as the sashes are lowered.

◆ Starting on one side of the window, remove the stop *(page 28)* and angle the lower sash inward out of the frame.

◆ Unhook the ends of the tape from both sides of the sash *(left)* and carefully feed them back into the tape balance drums.

◆ Remove the screws that secure the drums and pull them out of their pockets in the side or head jamb.

◆ Slip the new drums into the jambs and fasten them with wood screws.

◆ Pull the end of the tape from the drums with long-nose pliers and hook them to the sash.

◆ Angle the sash back into the window frame and replace the stop.

If you are replacing the drums for the upper sash, remove the lower sash first, then follow the steps above.

# CORD BALANCE REPAIRS

HEAD JAMB LINER

SIDE JAMB LINER

## 1. Pulling out the jamb liners.

◆ With both sashes at the bottom of the window frame, remove the two screws that fasten the vinyl liner to the head jamb and pull out the liner *(above, left)*. Then raise both of the sashes to the top of the frame.

◆ Remove the left liner, which generally is made in two sections. Unscrew the lower of the two pieces. Gently bend the bottom of this section of the liner toward the center of the window and pull the liner down and out *(above, right)*. The liner on the right side does not need to be removed.

CORD BALANCE

CORD

## 2. Replacing the balances.

Cord balances fit into pockets in each corner of the head jamb. Each balance contains one reel for the upper sash and one for the lower; a nylon cord runs from each reel to the side of a sash.

◆ Lower the bottom sash and angle the left side out of the window frame.

◆ Unhook the cord *(left)* and guide it up to its balance. Repeat the procedure with the cord on the right side and set the sash aside.

◆ Lower the upper sash, unfasten its cords the same way, and set it aside.

◆ Remove the two screws that secure each balance in its pocket in the head or side jamb and remove both balances.

◆ Install new balances, hooking their cords to each side of the top sash, then the bottom one.

◆ Reinstall the top sash by simply sliding it back up into place.

◆ To reinstall the bottom sash and liner, tilt the right side of the sash into the frame. Then, holding the liner against the edge of the sash, push the left edge of the sash and the liner together back into place, and screw the liner in position.

◆ Install the piece of the liner removed from the head jamb in Step 1 *(page 17)*.

# BLOCK-AND-TACKLE CHANNEL BALANCE REPLACEMENT

## Replacing the balance.

Inside this type of balance is a block-and-tackle mechanism (a cord with double pulleys). A hook at the end of the cord fits into a hole in the jamb. When the sash is lowered, the spring is put under tension.

◆ To remove the lower sash, flip up the clips holding the balances at the top of the jambs. (You may have to remove the interior stops first, unless you are working with vinyl windows, which have no interior stops). Raise the lower sash—the clips will disengage the balance from the sash—and remove it by pushing one side toward the jamb channel and swinging the other side out from the frame. (To remove the upper sash, lower it to expose the clips and remove it in the same way as the bottom sash.)

◆ Pull the bottom of each balance away from the jamb to expose its cord. Push the hook up and out and remove the balance *(right)*.

◆ To install the new balances, slide the top of one balance under the clip. Hold the balance with one hand, pull the cord, and hook it to the jamb. Repeat for the other side.

◆ Install the sash, then lower it to re-engage the balance, push the clips back in, and attach the stops, if necessary.

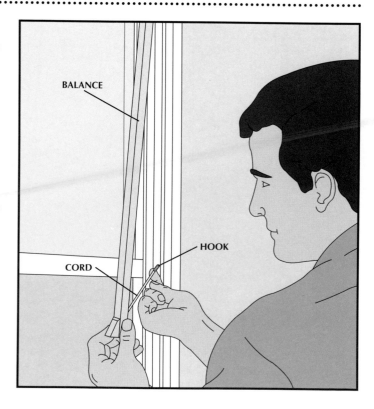

BALANCE

HOOK

CORD

A window sash designed to swing can stick in paint or dirt at its edges, but it can then be freed by the remedies on page 12. More often, it is the operating mechanism that moves the sash which binds, not the sash itself. You may be able to solve the problem by cleaning and lubricating the hinges and the moving parts *(below)*. Otherwise, you will have to repair or replace the mechanism.

**Working on the Operating Mechanism:** The operating mechanism for both casement and awning windows consists of a metal housing, a shaft with a crank handle at one end, and a worm gear at the other. An extension arm (or, in an awning window, two scissorlike arms) pivots in the housing at one end and is linked to the bottom of the sash at the other. When the crank is turned, teeth at the pivot end of the arm or arms mesh with the worm gear, swinging the arm—and the sash—in or out.

If the grease inside the operating mechanism is thick with dirt, you can clean and relubricate the gears. But if the gears have become so worn that they do not mesh, then you will have to replace the entire mechanism. The replacement must match the old mechanism exactly and, on a casement window, it must move the sash in the same direction as the old one. Most hardware stores stock some replacement operating mechanism, but you may have to order it from the window manufacturer or a specialty shop. If the crank handle turns without opening the window, the part needs to be replaced. It is secured by a setscrew and slides off its shaft.

**Solving Latch Problems:** A faulty latch can be replaced by removing the screws that fasten it to the jamb. If the latch fails to pull the sash tight to the weather stripping, you can shim the latch as you would a hinge *(page 25)*.

 **TOOLS**

Wire brush
Screwdriver
Pliers

 **MATERIALS**

Silicone spray
   lubricant
Petroleum jelly
Graphite powder

Kerosene
Replacement oper-
   ating mechanism
Replacement screws

## MAINTENANCE FOR SWINGING WINDOWS

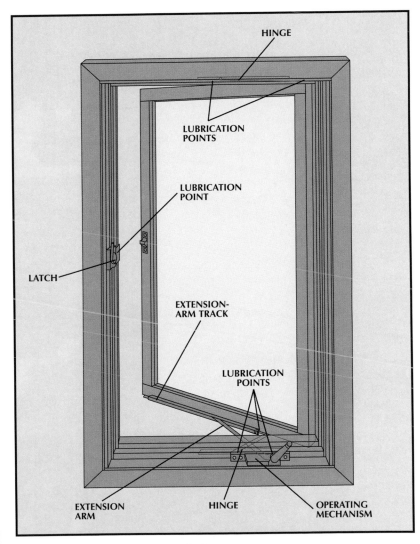

### Lubricating a casement window.
◆ Spray silicone lubricant on the hinges, the pivot point of the latch, and the joint between the crank handle and the operating mechanism.
◆ Open and close the window several times to work the lubricant into the joints.

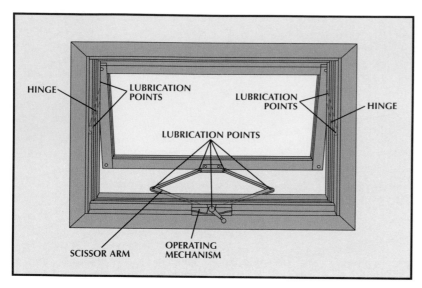

## Lubricating an awning window.

◆ Lubricate the hinges, the joints between the scissor arms and the sash, the pivot joint in the middle of each scissor arm, and the joint between the crank handle and the operating mechanism.

◆ Open and close the window several times to work in the lubricant.

## Cleaning an extension-arm track.

◆ Open the window fully and remove hardened grease, paint, and accumulated dirt from the track with a wire brush.

◆ Scrape away any remaining debris with a screwdriver, taking special care to remove obstructions inside the lip of the track.

◆ Coat the inside of the track with a thin layer of silicone spray lubricant.

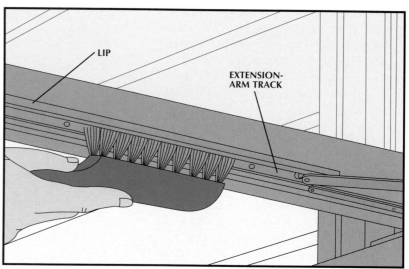

# RESTORING SMOOTH OPERATION TO CASEMENT WINDOWS

## 1. Unfastening the operating mechanism.

◆ Open the window and remove the screws that fasten the operating mechanism to the jamb; if the screws are not visible, pry off the stop above the operating mechanism (*inset*) by the method shown on pages 28 and 29 to gain access to them.

◆ On a casement window like the one pictured at right, remove any screws or spring clips that hold the extension arm in its track at the bottom of the sash.

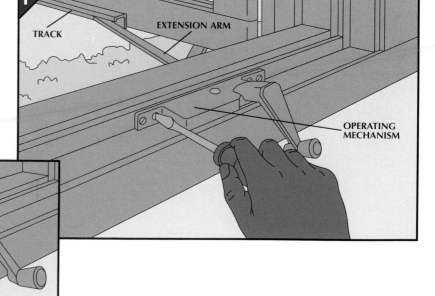

## 2. Removing the operating mechanism.

◆ Pull the crank mechanism inward, sliding the extension arm along its track until the end of the arm slips free. Pull the arm completely through its slot in the window frame.

◆ Inspect the gear on the extension arm. If the teeth are rounded or broken, install a new operating mechanism. Otherwise, wash the housing out with kerosene to remove the old grease and let the operating mechanism dry completely.

◆ Coat metal gears lightly with petroleum jelly or graphite powder and turn the crank handle several times to spread the lubricant. Do not lubricate nylon gears; if they are not working smoothly, replace the operating mechanism.

# SERVICING AN AWNING WINDOW

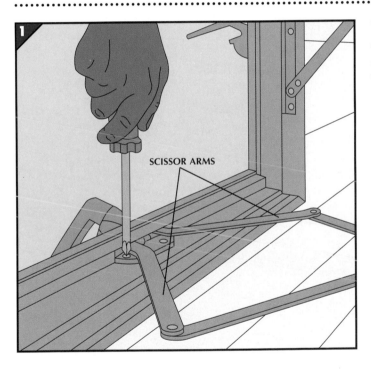

SCISSOR ARMS

## 1. Releasing the operating mechanism.

◆ Open the window as wide as possible. If the sash hinges are old and worn, brace the window with blocks of wood so the window will not slam shut when the scissor arms and operating mechanism are removed.

◆ Unscrew the mounting screws that secure the operating mechanism to the window frame *(left)*.

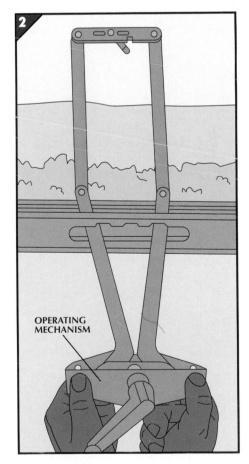

OPERATING MECHANISM

## 2. Replacing the operating mechanism.

◆ Reach under the sash and unhook the scissor arms from their clips on the sash. For scissor arms that are secured to the sash, remove the screws. If the window has extension arms that slide along a track on the sash, spread the arms and slide their shoes off each end of the track.

◆ Straighten the scissor arms and pull them clear of the window frame *(right)*.

◆ Clean and lubricate awning window operators as you would casement window operating mechanisms. If gears are worn or broken, replace the operating mechanism.

**D**oors often rattle, bind, or refuse to close. Rattles sometimes may be cured simply by installing weather stripping or repositioning the stops *(pages 28 and 32)*. Likewise, other simple repairs can improve a door's operation.

**Paint Problems:** Paint build-up can cause a swinging door to bind. Remove excess paint as you would for a sticking window *(page 11)*. If a door binds slightly at the top or bottom, plane or sand the point where it sticks *(pages 23-24)*; however, moisture can cause an unsealed door to swell, so paint or varnish any bare wood during a dry season.

**Adjusting Hinges:** Sometimes simply tightening the hinge screws will free a sticking door. If the screws turn but will not tighten, plug and redrill the holes *(page 24)*. When the door sticks along the lock side, recess the hinge leaves or remove the door and plane the hinge side. If the problem is at the top of the lock side, shim the bottom hinge *(page 25)* or cut a deeper mortise for the top hinge *(page 112)*. Use the reverse procedure on a door that binds at the bottom of the lock side.

**Warped Doors and Jambs:** On a warped interior door with two hinges, move the stop molding or the strike plate to accommodate the warp, then install a third hinge. Exterior doors generally must be replaced.

If the jamb bows outward, try the method shown on pages 25 and 26. To straighten a jamb that bows inward, adapt the procedure and place shims where needed. Do not try to straighten a bow of more than $\frac{1}{2}$ inch; instead, replace the jamb.

**Realigning the Lock:** When the bolt does not properly meet the strike, you can file the strike plate or reposition it *(page 25)*. If the hinges are too deeply recessed for the bolt to enter the strike, try placing cardboard shims beneath them.

**Jammed Sliding Doors:** Start by cleaning the track with a stiff brush and a vacuum cleaner. To replace broken rollers, you must remove the door. For a metal door, remove the bottom rail to get at the rollers *(page 27)*; rollers for wooden doors can usually be replaced without removing the rail. A slightly dented track can be straightened by hammering a block of wood into the track; a badly damaged track must be replaced *(page 27)*.

 **TOOLS**

| | |
|---|---|
| Tape measure | Mini-hacksaw |
| 2x4 or plywood straightedge | Utility knife |
| | File |
| Combination square | Jack plane |
| Hammer | Block plane |
| Mallet | Electric drill |
| Wood chisel | Counterbore bit |
| Handsaw | Pry bar |
| Hacksaw | Carpenter's nippers |
| | Locking-grip pliers |
| | Clamp |

 **MATERIALS**

| | |
|---|---|
| Wood dowel | Galvanized finishing nails ($3\frac{1}{2}$") |
| Galvanized flat-head wood screws ($2\frac{1}{2}$" No. 12) | Shims |
| | Sandpaper (medium grade) |
| | Carpenter's glue |

 **SAFETY TIPS**

*Protect your eyes with safety goggles when pulling nails.*

## The Use and Care of a Plane

✔ For smooth cutting, lubricate the bottom of the plane, called the sole, with wax.

✔ Work with the grain and remove the wood in several thin shavings.

✔ Apply pressure to the toe or front of the plane at the beginning of each stroke, then gradually shift the pressure to the heel, or back, as you finish the cut.

✔ To protect the plane iron —or blades—always place the plane on its side when the iron is exposed.

✔ After the job is completed, retract the plane iron completely.

✔ When the cutting edge becomes dull or nicked, remove and sharpen the iron.

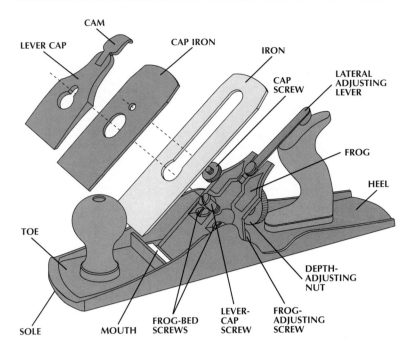

CAM
LEVER CAP
CAP IRON
IRON
CAP SCREW
LATERAL ADJUSTING LEVER
FROG
HEEL
TOE
SOLE
MOUTH
FROG-BED SCREWS
LEVER-CAP SCREW
FROG-ADJUSTING SCREW
DEPTH-ADJUSTING NUT

## Anatomy of a jack plane.

A jack plane is used for planing the edges or faces of wood. The iron—or blade—and cap iron, which prevents blade vibration, are fastened together with a cap screw to form a double iron that rests on a slanting piece called the frog. The lever cap and its cam fasten the double iron in place; locking pressure is adjusted by turning the lever-cap screw. On the sole of the plane, the mouth—the opening through which the iron projects—is adjusted by loosening two frog-bed screws and turning a frog-adjusting screw. For fine work move the frog forward; for coarse planing shift it back.

The cap iron should be set about $\frac{1}{16}$ inch behind the cutting edge of the iron for all-purpose planing; move it closer for fine jobs. The depth adjusting nut controls the depth of the cut the iron makes; the lateral adjusting lever aligns the iron's cutting edge parallel to the sole. A knob and a handle provide holds for two hands.

## Anatomy of a block plane.

A block plane is used for planing end grain. To that end, the single iron lies at a lower angle than the iron of a jack plane, and the bevel of the iron faces up. The lever-cap screw and the locking lever tighten the lever cap directly against the iron; a second lever, secured by a finger rest on the toe of the plane, adjusts the mouth. An adjusting nut controls the depth of the cut, and a third lever—the lateral adjusting lever—aligns the iron's cutting edge so it is parallel to the sole. On this small plane the vertical flanges, called wings, provide a handhold enabling you to operate the tool with one hand.

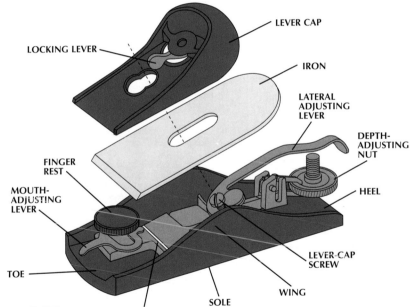

LEVER CAP
LOCKING LEVER
IRON
LATERAL ADJUSTING LEVER
DEPTH-ADJUSTING NUT
FINGER REST
MOUTH-ADJUSTING LEVER
HEEL
TOE
LEVER-CAP SCREW
MOUTH
SOLE
WING

DEPTH ADJUSTING NUT
LATERAL ADJUSTING LEVER
CORRECT ALIGNMENT

## Adjusting the plane iron.

Hold the plane—in this example, a jack plane—upside down over a light-colored background and sight along the sole. Turn the depth adjusting nut until the iron is at the desired depth of cut. If the iron projects unevenly across the width of the mouth, move the lateral adjusting lever to correct the alignment (inset).

## Planing the top or bottom of a door.

◆ To plane the top of a door, wedge the door halfway open. Lay a long, straight piece of lumber on the top edge of the door and mark any high points on the door.

◆ Hold a block plane by its wings, setting your index finger on the finger rest. Working from the sides of the door toward the center to avoid splintering, plane until there is $\frac{1}{8}$-inch clearance between the top of the door and the head jamb.

◆ To check for squareness, slide a combination square along the face and edge of the door, and mark and plane any remaining high points.

To plane the bottom of the door, remove it as described below and shave the bottom edge until there is $\frac{1}{8}$-inch clearance between the door and the floor.

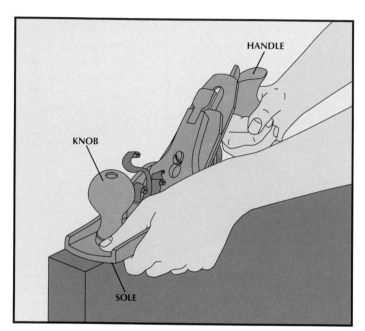

HANDLE

KNOB

SOLE

## Planing the hinge or lock side of a door.

If less than $\frac{1}{8}$ inch of material must be removed, plane the lock side of the door; otherwise, plane the hinge side. If you are planing the lock side, maintain the bevel *(page 116)*. When planing the hinge side, deepen the mortises if necessary before replacing the hinges.

◆ Starting with the bottom hinge and working up, take the door off the hinges by driving the pins up and out with a hammer and nail.

◆ Remove the hinges and support the door with a door jack *(page 116)* or have a helper hold it on edge.

◆ Mark the edge of the door as described above.

◆ Grip the handle of a jack plane with one hand. Hold the thumb of the other hand against the knob and curl your fingers under the sole and against the board as a guide. (If the wood is rough, grip the knob.)

# QUICK FIXES FOR DOORS

### Tightening loose screws.

◆ Remove the door as described above, then take off the hinge.

◆ Enlarge the holes so a dowel will fit tightly in them.

◆ Cut lengths of the dowel to serve as plugs, then coat them with glue and tap them into the holes *(right)*.

◆ Let the glue set for at least an hour, then drill pilot holes through the plugs and screw the hinges back in place.

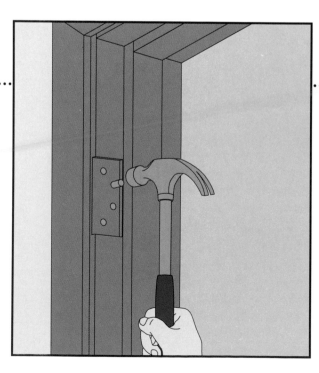

### Shimming a hinge.
◆ Wedge the door open.
◆ Loosen the screws that fasten the hinge leaf to the jamb.
◆ Insert a cardboard shim, slotted at the level of the screws, behind the hinge leaf, then tighten the hinge screws and test the door.
◆ Add a second shim if necessary.

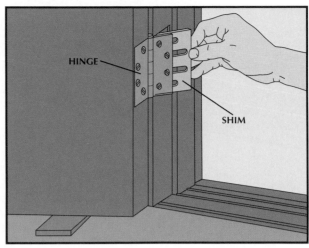

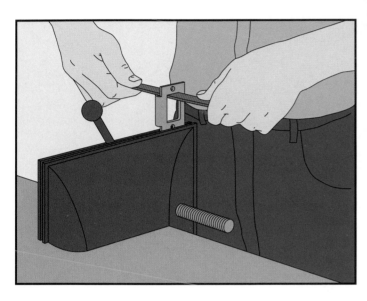

### Filing a strike plate.
◆ If a strike plate is less than $\frac{1}{4}$ inch out of alignment with the bolt, remove the plate and secure it in a vise.
◆ Enlarge the plate opening $\frac{1}{16}$ inch at a time with a flat double-cut file until the bolt fits.
◆ If necessary, enlarge the strike-plate hole in the jamb with a chisel.

For a larger misalignment, reposition the strike plate as described on page 119.

# STRAIGHTENING A JAMB

### 1. Marking the bow.
◆ For an exterior door *(right)*, remove the casing inside the house *(page 29)*. For an interior door, remove the casing on both sides of the partition.
◆ Wedge the door open.
◆ Hold a long, straight scrap of plywood against the jamb and mark the high point of the bow.

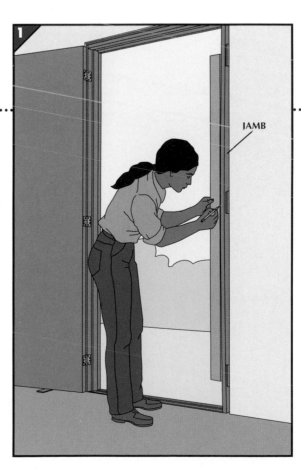

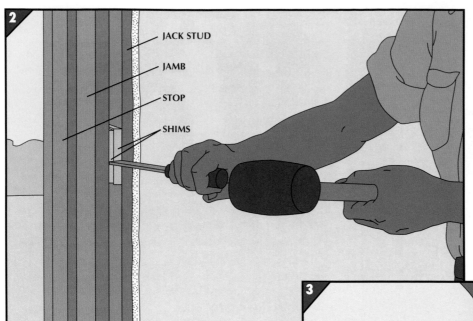

### 2. Removing the shims.

◆ Pry the entire length of the bowed jamb away from the jack studs just enough to loosen it.

◆ With a mallet and a $\frac{1}{4}$-inch wood chisel, split the shims that are nailed between the jamb and the jack stud and pull out the fragments. If the shims do not split easily, cut the nails with a mini-hacksaw *(page 37, Step 3)* or pull them out with carpenter's nippers *(page 29)*.

### 3. Eliminating the bow.

◆ At the high point of the bow, counterbore a pilot hole through the jamb for a $2\frac{1}{2}$-inch galvanized No. 12 flathead wood screw.

◆ Drive the screw through the jamb into the jack stud, tightening the screw until the jamb is straight.

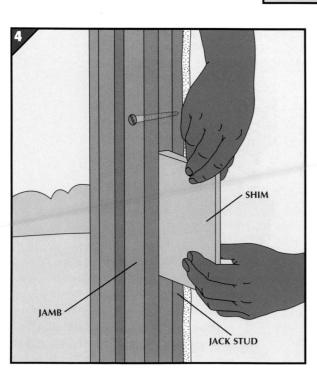

### 4. Reshimming the jamb.

◆ On an exterior door, insert the butt end of a shim between the jamb and the jack stud just below the screw used to straighten the jamb *(left)*.

◆ Cut 3 inches from the thin end of a second shim and tap it in alongside the first shim.

◆ Drive two $3\frac{1}{2}$-inch galvanized finishing nails through the jamb and shims into the jack stud.

◆ Install a pair of shims at the level of each of the shims on the opposite side of the door, and add two more pairs in the unshimmed spaces.

On an interior door, insert full-sized shims, thin end first, between the jamb and the jack stud from opposite sides of the jamb. Nail through the jambs and shims into the jack stud, then score the protruding ends of the shims with a utility knife, and break them off.

# REPLACING SLIDING DOOR ROLLERS

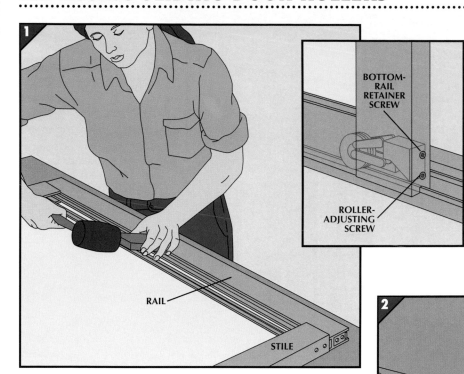

BOTTOM-RAIL RETAINER SCREW

ROLLER-ADJUSTING SCREW

RAIL

STILE

### 1. Removing the bottom rail.
◆ Dismount the door by lowering it with the roller-adjusting screws on the side or face of the door and tilting the door out of the opening.
◆ Lay the door on a flat surface, and undo the bottom-rail retainer screw *(inset)*.
◆ Clamp the door to a table and tap a wood block against the rail with a mallet to free the rail from the door *(left)*.

### 2. Installing new rollers.
◆ Clamp the bottom rail to a table and slide the worn or broken roller units out of the rail, prying with an old screwdriver if necessary.
◆ With a mallet, tap a new unit—rollers facing the middle of the door —into each end of the rail.

# A NEW CHANNEL FOR AN OLD TRACK

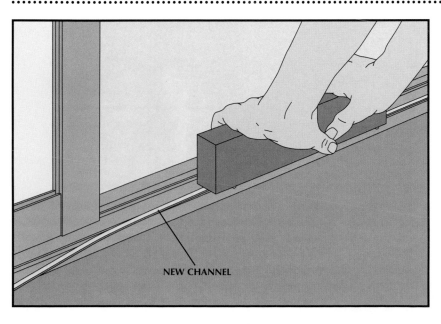

NEW CHANNEL

### Replacing the track channel.
◆ Remove the door as described in Step 1 above.
◆ Pull off the old channel with locking-grip pliers.
◆ With a hacksaw, cut a steel channel to the length of the dented track, then snap the channel onto the old track, pressing it down with a wood block *(left)*.
◆ Readjust the rollers *(page 106, Step 7)*.

# Replacing Door and Window Trim

Trim for a door or window serves many purposes. For example, the stops—the strips of trim inside the top and sides of the opening—keep a door or the sash of a casement window from swinging too far and help to seal gaps between the door or window and the jambs. The interior sill of a window—the stool—serves as a bottom stop; the exterior sill, called the finish sill, is angled to carry water away from the window, and also forms the base of the window frame, like a bottom jamb.

The illustrations on the following pages show the trim work on a door, but the instructions apply to both doors and windows. Removing the door before these repairs is optional but it may provide more working room.

**Buying Replacement Trim:** Lumberyards carry trim pieces in different shapes, thicknesses, and widths, but to match old trim, you will have to check secondhand building-supply yards. Otherwise, you may have to settle for the best match for the damaged piece from what is available and replace the other parts of the trim to match.

**Installing the Casing:** The position of the casing depends on the type of unit it surrounds. On doors and casement windows, the casing is normally set back from the inside edge of the jamb to avoid having to cut a notch to fit around the hinges.

Where pieces of casing meet, the joints are generally mitered. The top piece has two 45-degree miter cuts, which fit similar cuts at the tops of the side pieces. Some windows are cased like picture frames, with four casing strips miter-cut to 45-degree angles at the ends.

Stops, like casing, may be mitered. On molded stops, however, the best way to help prevent the joint from separating is to cope the side stops to fit the contour of the head stop *(page 33, Step 3)*.

## TOOLS

| | |
|---|---|
| Tape measure | Hammer |
| Combination | Nail set |
|   square | Putty knife |
| Utility knife | Miter box |
| Wood chisel | Dovetail saw |
| Pry bar | Coping saw |
| Carpenter's nippers | Block plane |
| Mallet | Sanding block |

## MATERIALS

| | |
|---|---|
| Casing stock | Sandpaper |
| Stop molding |   (medium grade) |
| Finishing nails | Wood putty or spack- |
|   ($1\frac{1}{2}$", 2") |   ling compound |

### SAFETY TIPS

*To protect your eyes when nailing trim or removing it above eye level, wear goggles.*

# REMOVING CASINGS AND STOPS

## 1. Removing the stops.
◆ Score the joints between the stops and the jambs with a utility knife to create a slight gap.
◆ Starting at the bottom of a side stop, set a chisel between the stop and the jamb, with the bevel of the chisel against the jamb. (To avoid ruining the sharp edges of a good chisel, use an old one.) Tap the chisel with a mallet, working up the stop to pry it away from the jamb.
◆ Repeat the procedure on the other side stop, then on the head stop.

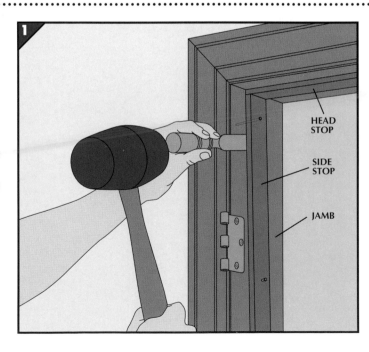

## 2. Prying off the casing.
◆ Remove the casing partway with a mallet and chisel, as for a stop, then insert the flat end of a pry bar behind the outer edge of the casing. Place a thin scrap of wood behind the bar to avoid marring the wall.
◆ Working up from the bottom of the side casing, slowly pry the casing completely free. Remove the other side casing and the head casing in the same way.

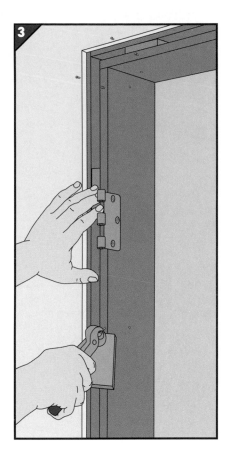

## 3. Extracting nails.
◆ If a finishing nail does not come out with the casing but remains embedded in the jamb or wall, grip the head with carpenter's nippers. Insert a piece of scrap wood under the tool to protect the jamb, then roll the nipper head against the wall to twist the nail free *(left)*.
◆ If the nail is in a stop or casing that you want to reuse, grip the shank of the nail protruding at the back of the stock with carpenter's nippers and pull the head completely through the piece.

# INSTALLING NEW CASINGS

## 1. Measuring the head casing.
◆ Around doors and casement windows, determine how far from the inside edge of the frame to set the casing—typically $\frac{1}{8}$ inch—to avoid having to cut around the hinges. (On some double-hung windows, you need not make these marks, because the casing is positioned flush with the inside of the jambs.)
◆ With a combination square, measure this distance from the inside edge of the jamb and mark the jambs at several points, taking care to show where the lines intersect at the corners *(left)*.
◆ Measure the distance between the setback marks on the side jambs at the top.
◆ Mark this distance on the thinner edge of a piece of casing and add twice the width of the stock to leave room for the miter cuts, which will fan outward from the marks.

## 2. Cutting the miters.

◆ Bolt a miter box to a workbench, place the casing flat-side down, and set the saw for a 45-degree angle of cut.

◆ Using long, even strokes, saw the strip on the outside edge of one of the marks you have made.

◆ Reverse the 45-degree angle and cut the second miter on the outside edge of the mark at the other end.

If you are working on a lot of trim, consider renting a power miter saw *(photograph)*. It makes quick work of mitering.

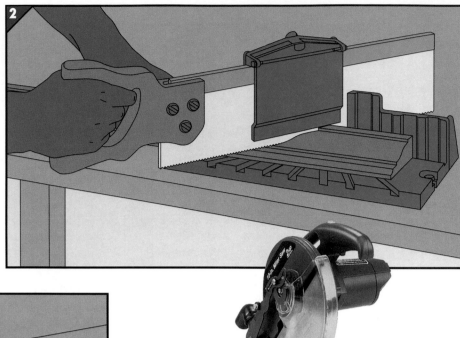

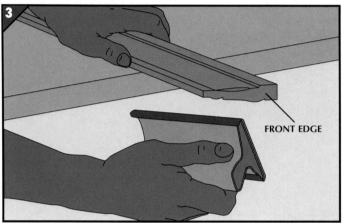

FRONT EDGE

## 3. Relieving the backs of the miters.

To make the joint fit snugly, sand the backs of the miters. Holding a sanding block fitted with medium-grade sandpaper at a slight angle to the edge of the stock, remove some of the wood, making sure you do not sand the front edge of the miter.

## 4. Nailing the top casing.

◆ Set the narrow edge of the casing at the marks on the jambs of doors and windows or at the corners of the jambs of double-hung windows with no setback, then tack the ends of the casing to the head jamb.

◆ Starting from one end of the casing, drive $1\frac{1}{2}$-inch finishing nails through the bottom of the workpiece into the jamb and 2-inch finishing nails along the outer edge of the casing into the header; space the nails at least 12 inches apart. Set the nails.

⚠ **CAUTION** *Never drive nails into casing at a sharp slant or you may pull the jamb out of alignment. On a double-hung window with sash pulleys and weight pockets (page 13) do not drive the nails into the pockets.*

## 5. Measuring the side pieces.

◆ For a door, measure the distance from the floor to the bottom of a miter in the top casing; for a window, measure from the stool. Add $\frac{1}{16}$ inch to this length and mark the total length on the thinner edge of a casing strip that is long enough to allow for an outward miter at one end. (The extra $\frac{1}{16}$ inch will allow you to remiter the casing if it does not fit perfectly.)

◆ Square off the strip at one mark and make a 45-degree outward miter cut from the other *(page 30, Step 2)*.

◆ Stand the side casing in place to check the fit of the miter; plane the side miter with a block plane if necessary and trim the casing to fit.

◆ Similarly mark, cut, and fit the other side casing.

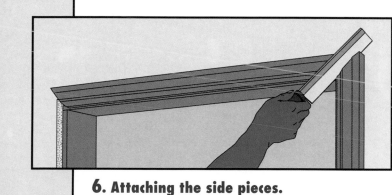

## 6. Attaching the side pieces.

◆ Align the miter joint and the edge of the casing with the setback marks you made in Step 1.

◆ Tack the side piece in position. Then, starting at the end of the piece, nail the casing to the jamb and the studs, using $1\frac{1}{2}$-inch finishing nails at the jamb and 2-inch finishing nails at the studs. Do not drive a nail at the location of the strike plate.

◆ If there is an uneven gap in a miter joint after the casing is nailed in place, you can improve the fit by cutting through the joint with a dovetail saw *(inset)*; the casing pieces are so flexible that lock-nailing *(Step 7, page 32)* will close the kerf left by the saw.

## 7. Lock-nailing the joints.

◆ Blunt the tips of 1½-inch finishing nails to prevent splitting the wood; alternatively, drill pilot holes.

◆ An inch from the outside corner of the casing, drive one nail through the top edge of the head casing into the side casing, and another horizontally through the edge of the side casing into the head casing *(right)*.

◆ If you intend to stain the trim, with a putty knife fill all nail holes in the casing with wood putty. Otherwise, use spackling compound.

# ADDING NEW STOPS

HEAD STOP

## 1. Positioning the head stop.

◆ With a miter box, cut stop molding to fit between the tops of the side jambs.

◆ Set the square edge of the stop against the closed door or sash and nail it in place temporarily with 1½-inch finishing nails.

For a double-hung window, the head stop fits against the closed sash and generally fills the space between the sash channel and the inside edge of the head jamb *(inset)*. On double-hung windows that slide in tracks *(page 15)*, set the stops against the raised edges of the tracks.

HEAD STOP

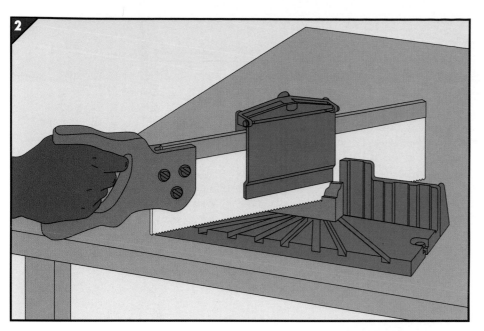

## 2. Cutting the side stops.

◆ For a door, cut two lengths of stop molding the same length as the distance from the head stop to the floor; for a window, measure to the stool.

◆ Flat stops can be butted up against each other; for contoured stops, cut a 45-degree miter across the molded face at the top end of each piece, angling from the molded face to the flat face that fits against the jamb *(left)*.

## 3. Coping the side stops.

◆ The mitered cuts made in the previous step will leave a scalloped profile on each molded face. Trace the profiles with a pencil and, following the marks, cut with a coping saw, angling the blade slightly to back-cut the piece a few degrees *(right)*. The ends of the coped side stop pieces will fit snugly against the head stop *(inset)*.

◆ Nail the side stops temporarily in place the same way you did when working on the head stop.

◆ If a door or a casement window binds or rattles against the tacked stops, move the stops for a better fit. Then secure all the stops with $1\frac{1}{2}$-inch finishing nails.

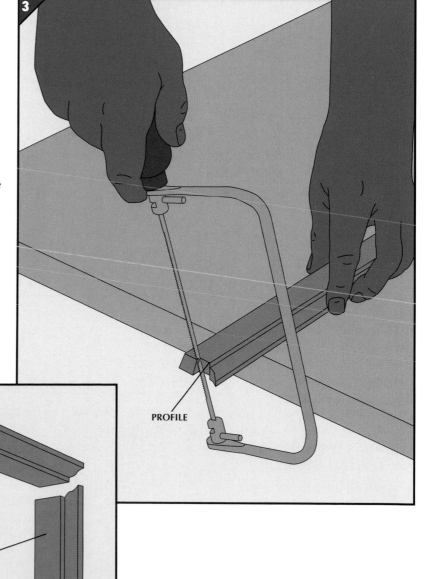

PROFILE

HEAD STOP

SIDE STOP

# Mending the Base of a Window

The parts of a window most vulnerable to damage and decay are the trim pieces at the base. Each has a special name *(opposite)* that can be confusing because the terminology is often mixed up in common usage. On a double-hung window, the finish sill is exposed outdoors only; the indoor "sill" is properly called a stool. Other types of windows generally have a sill but no stool.

The finish sill is usually the first piece to show signs of wear. If only the top surface is rotted, the damaged wood can be removed *(opposite)*. A badly rotted sill must be replaced. Purchase commercial sill stock as a replacement—you may need to order it from a contractors' supplier. If standard sill stock does not fit the dadoes in the window's jambs, have it specially milled.

Replacing a stool calls for a new piece that will fit your sill and walls—and these may vary from the modern standard. If your window needs a stool wider than the standard stock, either adapt the stock by gluing and tacking a strip of wood to the edge that fits against the window sash, or order a specially milled stool.

## TOOLS

| | |
|---|---|
| Tape measure | Plane |
| Combination square | Hammer |
| Awl | Mallet |
| Paint scraper | Pin punch |
|   or chisel | Nail set |
| Wood chisel | Saber saw |
| Pry bar | Circular saw |
| Flexible putty knife | Crosscut saw |
| Paintbrush | Miter box |
| Rasp | Coping saw |
| Sanding block | Mini-hacksaw |
| | Electric drill |
| | Caulking gun |

## MATERIALS

| | |
|---|---|
| Sill stock | Galvanized finishing |
| Stool stock |   nails ($2\frac{1}{2}$", 3") |
| Apron stock | Sandpaper |
| Shims |   (medium grade) |
| Finishing nails | Wood hardener |
|   ($1\frac{1}{2}$", 2") | Two-part epoxy |
| |   wood filler |
| | Caulk |

### SAFETY TIPS

*Protect your eyes with goggles when hammering, sanding, or prying window trim.*

## Choosing a Caulk to Keep out the Weather

The chart below lists the five types of caulk most often used outdoors. Water-base latex caulks are easier to clean up than the silicone and butyl varieties but may not last as long. Make certain the caulk you buy is compatible with the surfaces that straddle the joint you wish to seal.

| Type | Cleanup | Recommended surfaces | Pros and cons |
|---|---|---|---|
| Latex | Water | Glass, wood, metal | Paintable. Easy to apply and clean up. Available in colors. Apply in temperatures above 40°F. Limited flexibility; becomes brittle. Lifetime: 2-10 years. |
| Acrylic latex | Water | Glass, brick, wood, metal | Paintable. Easy to apply and clean up. Apply in temperatures above 40°F. Greater flexibility than latex caulk. Lifetime: 2-10 years. |
| Acrylic latex with silicone | Water | Glass, brick, wood, metal, concrete | Paintable. Available in colors, including clear. Apply in temperatures above 40°F. Stands up to weathering better than acrylic latex caulk. Lifetime: 5-15 years. |
| Silicone | Mineral spirits | Glass, wood, metal, concrete | Not paintable. Application temperatures vary by manufacturer. Excellent weathering characteristics. Fills large gaps better than latex caulks but tends to be more expensive. Lifetime: 10-50 years. |
| Butyl | Mineral spirits | Brick, wood, metal, concrete | Paintable. Inexpensive. Application temperatures vary by manufacturer. Good weathering characteristics; long-lasting, flexible. Hard to clean up; slow curing time. Lifetime: 2-10 years. |

## The base trim of a double-hung window.

A finish sill is seated in sloping dadoes—or grooves—in the side jambs *(inset)* that tilt the sill 15 degrees for drainage. Commercial sills have a drip groove under the outside edge to prevent water from creeping up the bottom of the sill and additional grooves to allow the wood to expand and contract. The inside edge is angled to make it vertical when the sill is installed. Outside, the finish sill rests on the rough sill. Sill horns fit against the outside edges of the jambs, providing a base for the exterior casing, or brickmold *(page 8)*. These horns need not extend farther than the outer edges of the brickmold. Inside, a stool fits over the finish sill, with stool horns generally extending $\frac{3}{4}$ inch beyond the edges of the interior casing. The bottom of the stool has a beveled rabbet angled to fit the sloping sill. An apron conceals the gap between the finish sill and the rough sill beneath it, and adds support to the stool. The interior stops seal the gap between the window and the jamb.

INTERIOR STOP

INTERIOR CASING

STOOL HORN

SILL HORN

JAMB

DADO

APRON

DRIP GROOVE

FINISH SILL

STOOL

ROUGH SILL

BEVELED RABBET

# REPAIRING A SILL

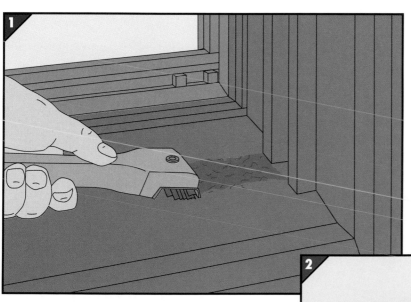

### 1. Scraping away damaged wood.

Rotted wood is gray and spongy. When probed with a sharp tool such as an awl, it crumbles, whereas sound wood cracks or splinters.

◆ With a scraper or chisel, carve out the rotted area until you reach undamaged wood *(left)*. Be sure to remove all the rot, even if you have to cut slightly into good wood.

◆ Apply a generous coat of wood hardener to all surfaces of the cavity with a brush or squeeze bottle and let it dry.

### 2. Filling the cavity.

◆ Mix two-part epoxy wood filler following the manufacturer's directions. These mixtures cure rapidly, so mix no more than you can apply in about 5 minutes.

◆ With a flexible putty knife, fill the cavity with the mixture, compressing it into all voids and cracks. Overfill the hole slightly and let the wood filler cure.

◆ Once it has dried, smooth the filler—first with a rasp, then with sandpaper—until the surface of the repair is smooth and flush with the surrounding wood.

◆ Prime the repair, then paint.

# PUTTING IN A NEW SILL

## 1. Removing the stool.

◆ Take off the interior side casings and stops *(page 28)*, pry off the apron with an old chisel or a pry bar, and raise the bottom sash.

◆ Check whether the stool has been nailed to the studs through the horns; if so, drive the nails through the stool with a pin punch.

◆ Outside the window, ease a pry bar between the stool and the sill, set a scrap of wood under the bar, and gently pry off the stool *(right)*.

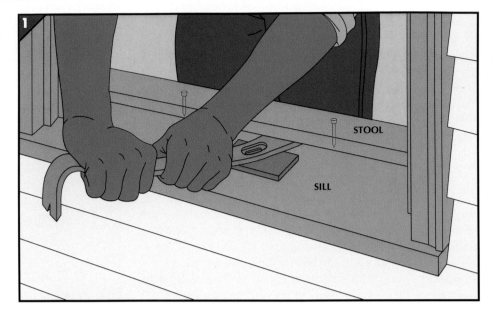

## 2. Removing the finish sill.

◆ Measure and take note of the exact distance between the side jambs, then make two cuts approximately a foot apart through the middle of the sill with a crosscut saw.

◆ Pry off the cut section and pull the end pieces out of their dadoes *(inset)*. The sill horns may be nailed to the brickmold. If so, separate the joint and sever the nails with a mini-hacksaw, or cut off the horns and remove them separately from the rest of the sill. Work slowly and carefully to avoid racking or splitting the jambs.

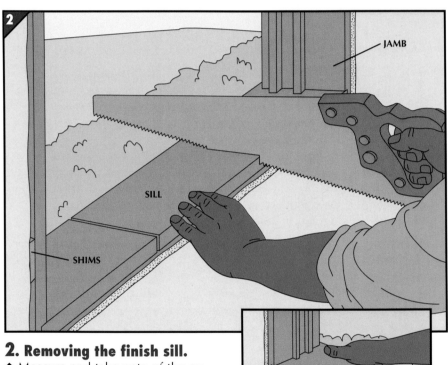

◆ Measure the distance between the jambs and compare with your original measurement. If the jambs have moved inward, check for shims behind them at the dado level. Add shims if necessary, then tap the jambs to the proper position with a hammer and a block of wood.

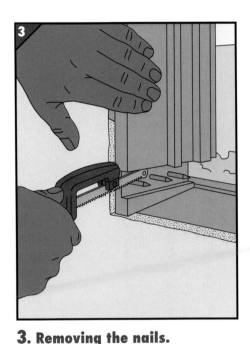

## 3. Removing the nails.

Working inside the house with a mini-hacksaw *(above)* or a hacksaw blade held in a gloved hand, cut off the ends of the nails that secured the sill inside the dadoes.

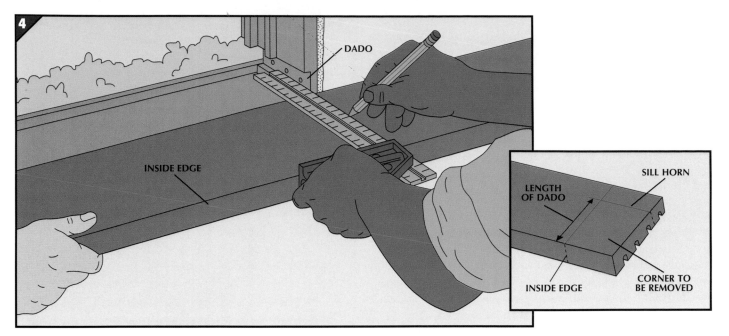

## 4. Cutting the new finish sill.

◆ Cut sill stock as long as the distance between the outer edges of the brickmolds.

◆ Working inside the house, have a helper center the piece—right side up with the inside edge toward the person—against the jambs, at the level of the dadoes. Set a combination square across the piece and into a dado and mark a line across the new sill for an exact fit inside the dado *(above)*; repeat for the other side.

◆ On each line, mark the length of the dado, measuring from the inside edge of the sill. Draw a perpendicular line from this mark to the end of the sill *(inset)*.

◆ With a saber saw, cut out the corners along the waste side of the lines, leaving the sill horns.

## 5. Installing the sill.

◆ Reaching outdoors, push the sill 1 or 2 inches into the dadoes in the jambs, then set a piece of scrap wood against the outside edge of the sill and tap lightly with a hammer until the inside edge of the sill is flush with the inside edges of the jambs.

◆ Inside the house, drill pilot holes through the corner of the sill into the side jambs and toenail the sill in place with $2\frac{1}{2}$-inch galvanized finishing nails *(inset)*.

◆ Drive the nail heads below the surface with a nail set.

◆ Outside the house, drill pilot holes straight through the front edge of the sill horns into the studs of the rough frame.

◆ Secure the sill horns with 3-inch galvanized finishing nails, then set the nails.

◆ Caulk all exterior joints, then fill the nail holes as you would for door trim *(page 32)*.

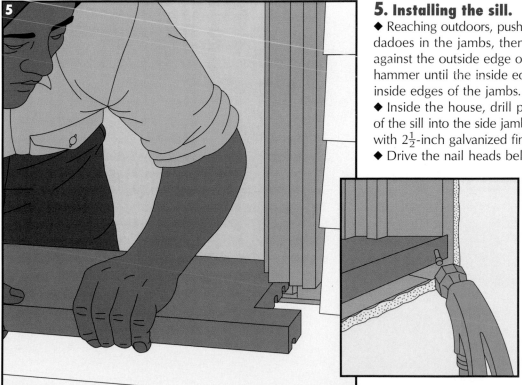

# FITTING A STOOL AND APRON

## 1. Marking the stool.
If your old stool is intact use it as a template to mark the new stool stock. Otherwise, follow these steps:
◆ To determine the length of the stool, measure the distance between the outer edges of the interior casings (their positions will be visible on the wall even though you have removed them) and add $1\frac{1}{2}$ inches to account for the $\frac{3}{4}$-inch overhang of the horns on both sides.
◆ To determine the width, measure the depth of the window from the inside edge of the jamb to the paint line marking the far edge of the interior stop. Add to this distance the thickness of the interior casing plus the $\frac{3}{4}$ inch that the horns will extend in front of the casing.
◆ Cut stool stock to this length and width. If you are using a circular saw, cut about $\frac{1}{4}$ inch outside your marks, and then plane the board down to the lines.
◆ Have a helper center the stool piece—right side up, inner, molded edge toward the person—against the jambs and level with the finish sill.
◆ Set the blade of a combination square across the stool piece and against the inner face of each side jamb. Draw lines from the jamb faces across the stool (right).
◆ At each end of the stool, starting directly above the inner corner of the rabbet on the stool's underside, draw a line that intersects the jamb line at a right angle (inset).
◆ Cut out corners on the waste sides of the lines.

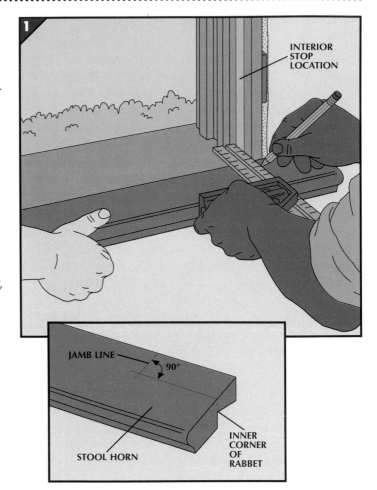

## 2. Attaching the stool.
◆ Slip the stool into position, with its rabbet fitted to the top corner of the sill, and close the window sash. There should be a $\frac{1}{16}$-inch gap between the sash and the stool; if the clearance is less than this, plane the stool down and sand the planed area smooth.
◆ Finish the ends of the horns as shown on the opposite page.
◆ Where the edge of the stool will be covered by the side stops, and at two points to the left and right of the center of the stool, drill pilot holes and drive $2\frac{1}{2}$-inch galvanized finishing nails through the stool into the sill (left).
◆ Drive the nail heads below the surface with a nail set.
◆ Replace the casings and the stops or cut new ones (pages 29-33).

## 3. Installing the apron.

◆ Cut a piece of apron stock that is $1\frac{1}{2}$ inches shorter than the stool, and finish the ends as shown *(below)*.

◆ Center the apron under the stool and drive three 2-inch finishing nails along the top of the apron—one at the center and one at each end—and three $1\frac{1}{2}$-inch nails similarly spaced along the bottom.

◆ Set the nails and fill the nail holes *(page 32)*.

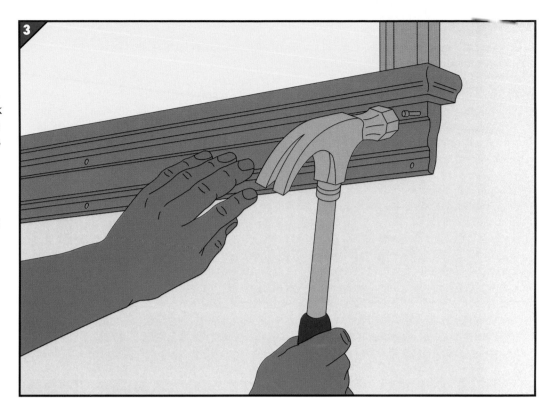

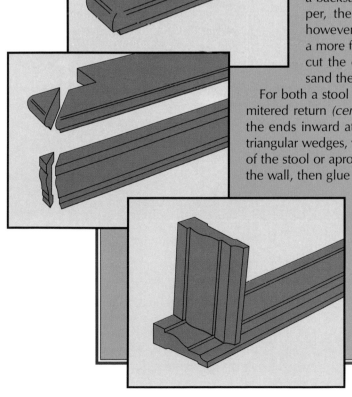

### ROUNDED, MITERED, AND COPED ENDS

You can simply square the ends of a stool or apron with a backsaw and miter box, smooth the cuts with sandpaper, then nail the piece in place. Most professionals, however, prefer to use techniques that give the window a more finished appearance. For a stool, one option is to cut the ends square, then round them with a rasp and sand them smooth *(top)*.

For both a stool and an apron, a more elaborate technique is the mitered return *(center)*. Cut the stool or apron to length and miter the ends inward at 45 degrees. Cut two scrap pieces of trim into triangular wedges, with a miter cut at one end to fit the mitered end of the stool or apron and a square cut at the other end to fit against the wall, then glue and nail the wedges in place.

A third finishing method, which is used for an apron with a molded pattern on its face, is to cope the ends to the same profile as the face. Cut the apron about an inch too long at each end and mark the correct end positions on the face. Set a scrap piece of apron stock on end at the marks *(bottom)* and trace the profile of the piece; then cut the apron along the traced line with a coping saw, keeping the saw vertical, and smooth the cut ends of the apron with sandpaper.

# Prescriptions for Damaged Screens

**E**ach of the two most common screening materials, aluminum and fiberglass, has its advantages. Aluminum is less likely to tear or sag, but unlike fiberglass it may corrode or oxidize. To restore rusted screening to its original condition, rub it with a wire brush, then vacuum it.

**Simple Repairs:** Repairing a very small hole may mean simply pushing the wires of the screening back into line with the tip of an awl. Other small gaps can be plugged with dabs of weatherproof glue or with patches glued in place. On aluminum screening you can fasten patches by weaving the wires at the edges of the patch into the surrounding mesh, or you can use ready-made patches with edging wires prehooked to clip onto the screening. On fiberglass screening, simply set a fiberglass patch over the hole, cover the patch with a cotton rag, and run a hot iron over the rag, fusing the patch to the screening.

**Replacing the Screening:** If the holes are too large to patch, or so close to the frame that the screening sags, replace the screening. On all metal frames and some wooden ones, screening is secured with a spline *(below)*—a thin strip pressed down over the screening and into a channel at the inside edges of the frame. To replace the screening, you must pull out the old spline and screening, then put a spline back in place over new screening *(opposite)*.

On some wooden frames the screening is secured with tacks or staples. New screening is installed while the frame is bowed by clamps *(page 42, Step 2)*. When the clamps are released, the frame tightens the screening as it straightens out.

Loose joints on wooden frames can easily be reinforced with corrugated fasteners, angle plates or screws.

 **TOOLS**
| | | |
|---|---|---|
| Tape measure | Awl | Screen-spline roller |
| Hammer | Heavy-duty shears | Hand stapler |
| Screwdriver | Tin snips | C-clamps |
| Wire brush | Utility knife | |

 **MATERIALS**
Brads ($\frac{3}{4}$")
Screening
Screen splines

## A SPLINE FOR SCREENING ON A CHANNELED FRAME

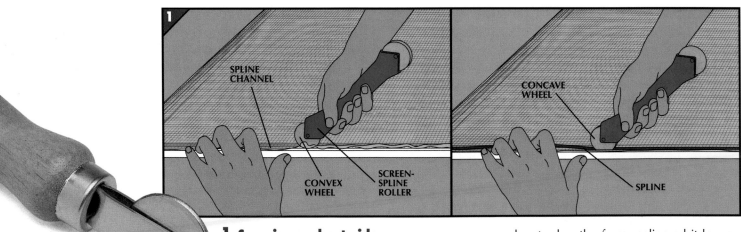

### 1. Securing a short side.
◆ With heavy-duty shears or tin snips, cut a piece of screening to the outer dimensions of the frame.
◆ If your screening is aluminum, crease it into the spline channel on a short side of the frame *(above, left)*, using the convex wheel of a screen-spline roller *(photograph);* start at a corner and work in short back-and-forth strokes.
◆ Set the old spline in place, or if it is dam-aged, cut a length of new spline a bit longer than the channel. With the concave wheel, force the spline into the channel over the screening *(above, right)*. Cut new spline at the corners of the frame and tamp it into place with a screwdriver.

If you are installing fiberglass screening which will not crease, roll the spline over the screening in one step.

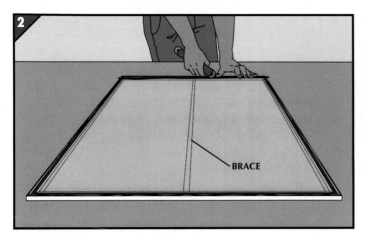

## 2. Completing the splines.
◆ Pull the screening taut at the opposite side of the frame, crease it if necessary, and roll a length of spline over it and into the channel *(above)*. If the frame bows inward, fit a board as a temporary brace to hold the sides parallel.
◆ With the screening pulled flat across the frame, add splines to the two remaining sides.

## 3. Trimming the excess screening.
With a utility knife, cut through the screening along the outer edges of the spline channels; slant the blade toward the outside of the frame to avoid cutting into the spline.

# STAPLING SCREENING TO A WOODEN FRAME

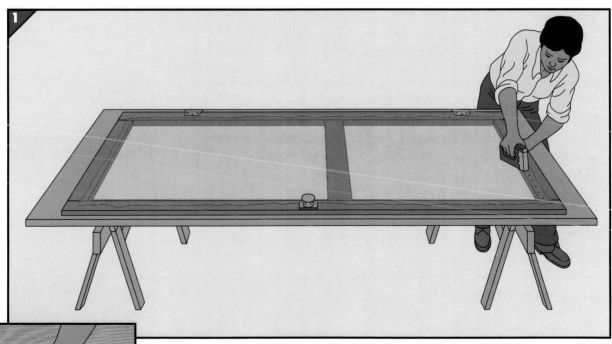

## 1. Fastening the first side.
◆ For aluminum screening, cut the material 2 inches larger than the frame opening.
◆ Staple the screening to a short side of the frame at 2-inch intervals, starting at a corner *(above)*. Angle each staple so it straddles several strands of the mesh.

For fiberglass screening, cut the material $\frac{1}{2}$ inch larger than the outside edges of the molding that will conceal the staples. To keep the screening from tearing along the line of staples, make a hem by folding the extra $\frac{1}{2}$ inch over as you staple the material *(inset)*.

$\frac{1}{2}$ INCH HEM

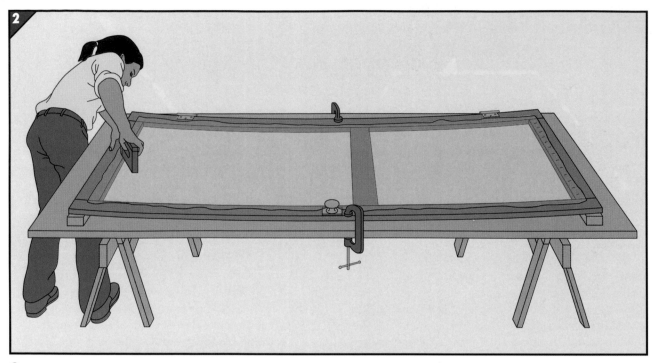

## 2. Attaching the remaining sides.

◆ Set blocks of scrap wood under the short sides of the frame and use a pair of C-clamps to force the centers of the long sides down about $\frac{1}{4}$ inch.

◆ Pull the screening taut along the unstapled short side, staple it and release the C-clamps.

◆ Staple the long sides, which are now stretched taut.

◆ Replace the molding, fastening it with $\frac{3}{4}$-inch brads every 6 inches.

◆ On metal screening, trim off the excess screening with a utility knife; the hem on fiberglass screening will be covered by the molding.

**TRICKS OF THE TRADE**

### Stretching Screening

The setup shown at left is an alternative to bowing the frame to stretch the screening. Cut the screening a few inches longer than the size of the frame. After stapling one end of the material to the frame, staple the other end to a board held against the frame. Then push down on the board as you staple the screening in place.

# Repairing and Installing Interior Shutters

Interior shutters are designed to open and close and usually have adjustable louvers. The louvers may need to be reattached to the rod that tilts them and the pegs that hold the louvers may break and need to be replaced. If the frame of a shutter comes unglued it can be clamped and reglued using bar clamps *(page 45)*.

**Fixing Sags:** Shutters tend to droop with time. To prevent this, fasten thin rubber bumpers to the bottom of each panel, so that the window stool or sill helps the hinges support the closed shutters. Use white bumpers to avoid smudging. To fix a sagging shutter, remove it and tighten the hinge screws in the same way as for a door *(page 24)*.

**Installing Interior Shutters:** You can have new shutters made to fit your windows, but it is cheaper to buy stock shutters oversized and trim them to fit as explained on page 45. Shutters can be hung either from the window casings or jambs. The casing installation method is easier because the shutters do not have to fit exactly. However, the jamb installation method shown here produces a neater appearance, since the shutters fit inside the window opening rather than protruding into the room. The jamb surface must be at least $1\frac{1}{4}$ inches to accommodate the hanging strip; if you do not have enough room, hang the shutters from the window casing.

 **TOOLS**

Tape measure
Straightedge
Hammer
Screwdriver
Long-nose pliers
Wrench
Utility knife
Bar clamps
Hand-screw clamps
Awl
Electric drill
Circular saw
1x4 guide strip
Sanding block
Plane

 **MATERIALS**

1x2s
2x4s
Common nails ($2\frac{1}{2}$")
Sandpaper (medium grade)
Carpenter's glue
U-shaped pins
Replacement aluminum loop strip
Replacement pegs and springs
Hinges and screws
Hook-and-knob latch

 **SAFETY TIP**

*Wear goggles when sawing to keep your eyes free of sawdust.*

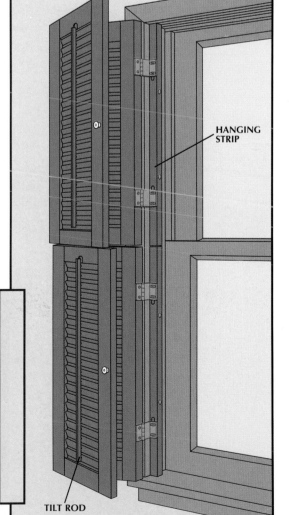

HANGING STRIP

U-SHAPED PINS

PEG

SPRING

TILT ROD

## Anatomy of an interior shutter.

Each shutter panel at left consists of a glued frame and a set of movable louvers; other types have fixed louvers. In each tier, the panels are hinged to each other; the panel at the window edge is also hinged to a hanging strip that is attached to the window jamb. Pegs fitted into holes in the shutter frame support movable louvers. Compression springs in the holes at the ends of the louvers *(inset)* hold them at the angle set by a tilt rod, which is attached to all the louvers either by a set of U-shaped pins or by a hooked aluminum strip.

# FIXING PINS, PEGS, AND JOINTS

## Attaching louvers to a tilt rod.

◆ If the louvers are held to the tilt rod with U-shaped pins—also known as staples—set the louvers individually to a horizontal position and turn the tilt rod sideways to expose the pins.

◆ To install a new pin in the louvers, dab carpenter's glue on the ends of the pin. Hold the louvers in place with the fingers of one hand, then push the new pin through the rod pin with long-nose pliers and into the louver pinholes *(right)*. Replace a rod pin in the same way, but loop it through the louver pin.

To fix a one-piece, hooked aluminum strip set in a wooden shaft *(inset)*, bend all the hooks open with long-nose pliers and remove the tilt rod.

◆ Pull the strip out of its channel in the rod and slide a new strip into place.

◆ One by one, bend the loops over the louver pins.

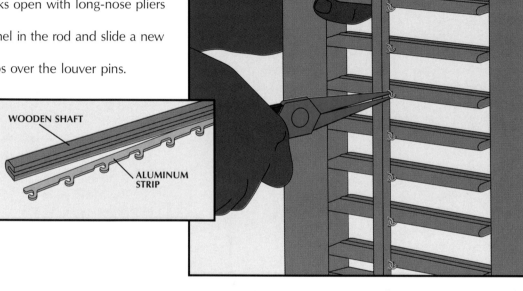

WOODEN SHAFT

ALUMINUM STRIP

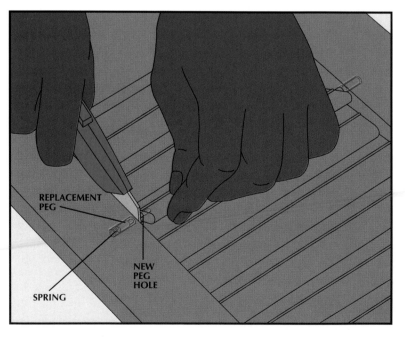

REPLACEMENT PEG

NEW PEG HOLE

SPRING

## Treating a broken louver peg.

Special replacement pegs have a narrow end to fit into the stub of the old peg.

◆ Take the shutter off its hinges, then unhook the louver from the tilt rod and pull it out of the shutter frame.

◆ Drill a $\frac{1}{8}$-inch-diameter hole in the peg stub remaining in the louver.

◆ If the spring and peg have fallen out of the end opposite the broken peg, replace them and fit the end of the louver over the peg.

◆ On the side with the broken peg, insert a replacement peg, wide end first, into the hole in the frame, holding the peg flush to the edge of the frame with a utility knife.

◆ Align the louver with the replacement peg, and slide the knife out *(left)*; the spring will push the narrow end of the replacement peg partway into the new hole in the peg stub.

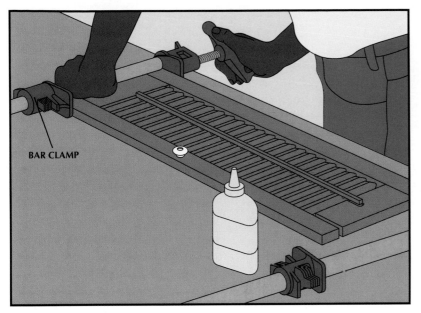

**BAR CLAMP**

### Gluing loose joints.
◆ With the panel off its hinges, clamp the end opposite the loose joint to keep it from opening when the other end is clamped *(left)*.
◆ Check the fit of the louver pegs in the sides of the frame and replace any compression springs that may have fallen out *(opposite page)*.
◆ Separate the loose joint slightly with a utility knife and scrape off the old glue.
◆ Push the frame together, leaving just enough space for the tip of a glue dispenser, and coat both sides of the loose joint with carpenter's glue.
◆ Clamp the frame tightly, using a second clamp at the glued end, and wipe off excess adhesive immediately. Leave the clamps in place until the glue dries—usually overnight.

# PUTTING UP A SET OF SHUTTERS

### CALCULATING HOW MUCH TO TRIM SHUTTERS

Because few windows are perfect rectangles, measure the length and width of each at three equidistant points, checking width between side jambs and height between the stool and the head jamb. Use the smallest measurement of length and width in the following calculations:

Subtract $\frac{7}{16}$ inch from the width of the opening to allow for panel hinges and hanging strips. Subtract $\frac{3}{8}$ inch from the height for clearance between the shutters and the window frame; if you install two horizontal tiers of shutters, subtract another $\frac{3}{16}$ inch from the total height for clearance between tiers. Divide the final height figure by the number of top and bottom edges (two in a single-tier installation, four in a double-tier); divide the final width figure by the number of vertical panel edges. The resulting figures indicate the amount to trim from the height and width of each panel for a perfect fit. Generally, you can trim up to $\frac{1}{2}$ inch from the side of a panel and as much as 2 inches from the top or bottom without weakening joints.

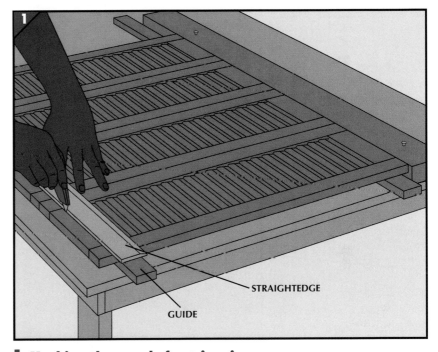

**STRAIGHTEDGE**

**GUIDE**

### 1. Marking the panels for trimming.
◆ Align a complete set of shutter panels, interior side down, across two 1-by-2s on a workbench, butting the ends against a 2-by-4 fastened to the bench with $2\frac{1}{2}$-inch nails.
◆ Use a pencil to mark the panels for trimming *(box)*, set a straightedge at the pencil marks, and score the shutters along the straightedge with a utility knife. Score the opposite ends of the panels in the same way, but score the side edges of each panel individually.

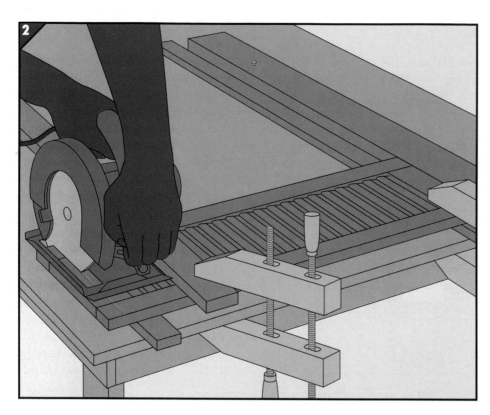

## 2. Trimming the panels.

◆ Clamp each panel over the 1-by-2s and anchor a 1-by-4 guide strip to the panel with a clamp at each end.

◆ Saw along the strip with a circular saw and sand the edges. To remove less than $\frac{1}{8}$ inch, use a plane. Trim the vertical edges in the same way.

◆ Cut the hanging strips to match the height of the panels.

## 3. Hinging the panels.

◆ Install the hinges on a hanging strip, placing each hinge-adjustment screw in the center of the vertical slot *(inset),* then tighten the screw while holding the nut with a wrench.

◆ Hold the strip against the back of the panels to be hinged and mark the locations of the hanging-strip hinges on the adjoining edges of the panels *(right).*

◆ Tape a penny between the panels near each hinge position to allow for clearance, then align connecting hinges, pin sides up, with the marks you have made. Mark the screw holes deeply with an awl to make pilot holes.

◆ Screw on the connecting hinges.

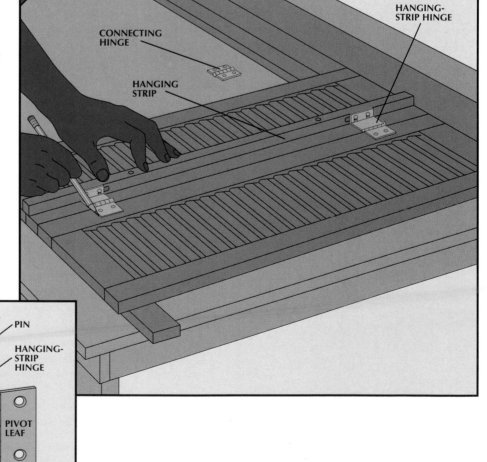

CONNECTING HINGE

HANGING STRIP

HANGING-STRIP HINGE

PIN

HANGING-STRIP HINGE

NUT

PIVOT LEAF

ADJUSTMENT SCREW

## 4. Fitting the hanging-strip hinges.

◆ Position the hanging strip under the end panel, lining up the top and bottom with the panel; mark the locations of the hanging-strip hinges on the panel edge *(right)*.

◆ Detach the pivot leaves from the hinges by pulling out the pins, then set each leaf at the pencil marks, placing it flush with the back edge of the panel so that the pin side is toward the interior edge of the panel. Mark the locations of the screw holes deeply with an awl, and screw the pivot leaves to the panels.

◆ Reassemble the hinges.

◆ With a helper, hold each half of the shutter set against the window opening and check all clearances. Detach the shutters from the hanging strips and plane the shutters where necessary.

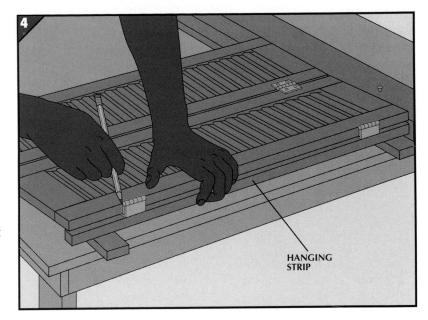

HANGING STRIP

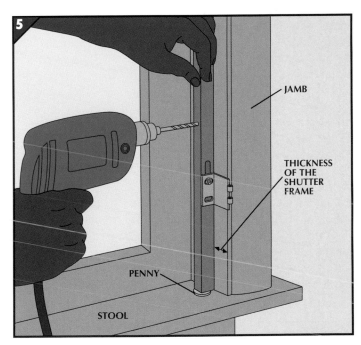

JAMB

THICKNESS OF THE SHUTTER FRAME

PENNY

STOOL

## 5. Installing the hanging strips.

◆ With a penny spacer between the bottom of the hanging strip and the stool, place each strip the thickness of the shutter frame back from the edge of the jamb. Drill through the mounting holes in the strip into the jamb.

◆ Fasten the hanging strips to the jamb with the screws that are provided by the manufacturer.

◆ Reattach the shutters.

## 6. Adjusting the shutters.

◆ Starting with the lower tier of shutters, close the two panels and note the gap between them and between the shutters and the stool.

◆ Open the shutters and loosen the adjustment screw and nut in each hinge on the hanging strip. Move the hinges vertically or horizontally to align the shutters, and tighten the screws.

◆ Adjust the panels to obtain an even gap the thickness of a penny between them and between the shutters and the stool. Adjust the upper tier in the same way.

◆ Drill a pilot hole and run a screw through the empty slot in each hanging-strip hinge and into the hanging strip.

◆ Install the hook-and-knob latch according to the manufacturer's instructions.

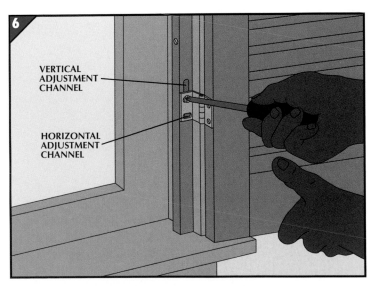

VERTICAL ADJUSTMENT CHANNEL

HORIZONTAL ADJUSTMENT CHANNEL

# The Glazier's Craft: Cutting and Setting Glass

**W**indows are glazed either with a single pane of glass, or with double or triple panes for increased insulation. Shown here are techniques for replacing both types. The same techniques can be used to refit single-pane windows with insulating panes; but these require a sash channel at least 1 inch wide.

**Measuring the Glass:** To determine the size of a single replacement pane, measure the inside of the frame after you have removed the old pane and putty, then subtract $\frac{1}{8}$ inch from each dimension to allow for expansion. Single-glazed panes will be cut to size by most glass and hardware stores, but you can do it yourself if the glass is less than 4 feet long. Insulating panes come in a range of pre-cut sizes; panes smaller than 12 by 12 inches generally must be custom-made. For the correct size of a replacement, consult a window dealer.

**Installing the Glass:** Before you cut a windowpane, practice on a piece of scrap glass to get a feel for the amount of pressure needed to score the glass for a clean cut. A rasping sound as you draw the cutter across the glass indicates that the pressure is right.

Single-pane glass is held in a wood frame with wedge-shaped glazier's points. With steel frames, spring clips or rubber gaskets are used. For panes secured with points or springs, glazing compound cushions the glass and forms a watertight seal.

Insulating glass is generally held in place by wood moldings in wood windows and by plastic moldings in aluminum or vinyl windows. If the glass is foggy the seal is broken and the unit must be replaced. Use a latex-based compound to glaze insulated glass—oil-based compounds will rot the sealant that holds the panes together.

 **TOOLS**

Tape measure
Straightedge
Wood chisel
Stiff-bladed putty
 knife
Utility knife

Wire brush
Small paintbrush
Long-nose pliers
Glass cutter
Dowel
Nipping pliers
Saber saw
Heat gun

 **MATERIALS**

Linseed oil
Light machine oil
Sandpaper (coarse
 grade and 240-grit
 silicon-carbide)
Emery stone
Galvanized finishing
 nails ($1\frac{1}{4}$")
Duct tape

Hardboard
Replacement glass pane
 or insulating glass unit
Glazier's points
Glazing compound
Silicone caulk
Replacement gasket for
 steel windows
Replacement moldings
 for metal or vinyl
 windows

 **SAFETY TIPS**

*Wear heavy leather work gloves when handling loose panes or fragments of glass. If you are removing broken glass or cutting glass, protect your eyes with safety goggles. When using solvent-base glazing compound instead of a water-base or acrylic compound, wear rubber gloves.*

---

## Tips for Handling Glass

Working with glass is not dangerous if you take the following precautions:
✔ Work with a helper whenever you carry panes larger than 4 by 4 feet.
✔ Transport glass flat in several layers of newspaper or blankets on a padded surface (an old rug or piece of carpet will do).
✔ Have a professional deliver any glass pane you cannot lay flat in your car.
✔ Cut glass on a padded surface.
✔ Immediately after cutting glass, sweep up any fragments left from the work.
✔ If the window is hard to reach, remove the sash *(page 13)* and do the work on a flat surface.
✔ Before storing panes, mark them with a grease pencil or masking tape so they are easily seen.

## 1. Removing broken glass.
◆ Tape newspaper to the inside of the sash to catch glass fragments.
◆ From outside the house, work the shards of glass back and forth to free them. If the glass is only slightly cracked, tap it lightly with a hammer to break it.

## 2. Scraping off the glazing compound.
◆ Brush the old glazing compound with linseed oil to soften it.
◆ Let the oil soak in for a half hour, then scrape off the softened compound with an old chisel or a stiff-bladed putty knife.
◆ If oil does not soften the compound sufficiently, warm it with a heat gun *(photograph)* on a low setting. Be careful not to heat surrounding panes as this could crack them.

> ⚠️ **CAUTION** *Old glazing compound may contain lead. When removing it, take the same precautions you would with lead paint* (page 10).

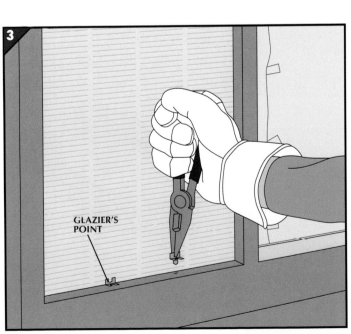

GLAZING COMPOUND

GLAZIER'S POINT

## 3. Smoothing the channel.
◆ Pull the glazier's points out of the frame with long-nose pliers and remove loose fragments of glass and glazing compound with a wire brush.
◆ Sand the channel smooth with coarse sandpaper and brush it with linseed oil. (Uncoated wood draws oil from the glazing compound and makes it brittle.)

# CUTTING A RECTANGULAR PANE

## 1. Scoring the glass.

◆ Lay the glass on a solid surface. Brush linseed oil or light machine oil on the area to be scored, or dip the cutter in the lubricant.

◆ Set a straightedge along the cut line. Holding a glass cutter vertically between your first and second fingers, start as close as possible to the far end of the glass and run the cutter along the straightedge and right off the near edge in one smooth motion. Do not score the line a second time—this will cause the glass to break with an uneven edge.

◆ Proceed directly to Step 2 because the scored line can begin to "heal" in humid air.

## 2. Snapping the glass.

◆ Do not tap the score line with the ball on the end of the glass cutter— this can chip the glass. Place a rod, such as a dowel—smaller in diameter than a pencil and at least as long as the score line—on the work surface. Position the score line directly over the rod and press down firmly on both sides of the score to snap the glass cleanly.

◆ Use 240-grit silicon-carbide sandpaper or an emery stone to smooth the new edge.

### MAKING A CLEAN BREAK

Running pliers *(right)* are an alternative to the dowel method for breaking glass shown in Step 2. On the outside of one jaw is a white guideline indicating the position of a ridge inside the jaw. To use the pliers, fit a pane of glass between the jaws, with the ridge at a line scored with a glass cutter. Squeeze the handles to snap the glass.

# A TEMPLATE FOR A CURVED CUT

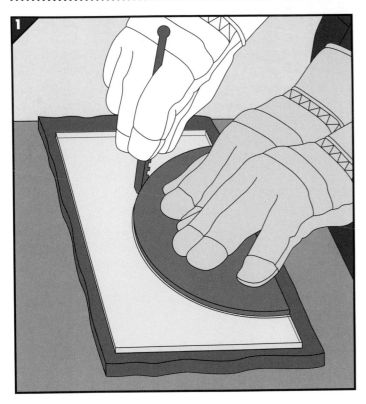

### 1. Making the score.
◆ Cut a hardboard template with a saber saw to the desired shape of the pane and set it on the glass. If the curved design has one straight edge, align the template's straight side with the edge of the glass.
◆ Set the glass on a soft pad. While a helper holds the template firmly with both hands, make the score in a single motion from one end of the curve to the other *(left)*.

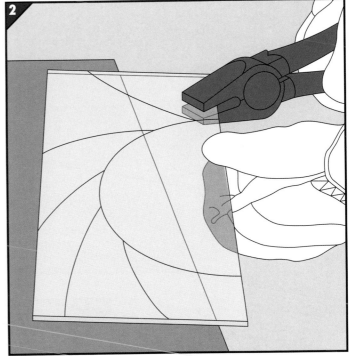

### 2. Snapping the curve.
◆ Scribe several radiating score lines from the curve to the edge of the glass.
◆ Hold one edge of the glass over the end of the worktable and snap off the scored segments with nipping pliers *(right)*.
◆ Smooth the edge with 240-grit silicon-carbide sandpaper or an emery stone.

# SETTING A SINGLE PANE IN A WOOD FRAME

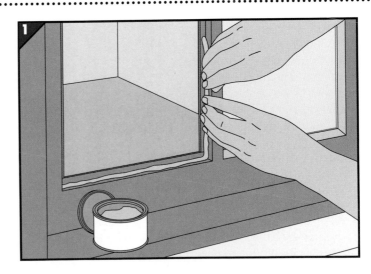

### 1. Lining the frame.
◆ Outside the house, roll glazing compound between your palms into strips about $\frac{1}{4}$ inch thick and press it into the channels in which the pane of glass will rest.
◆ Add compound until you have filled the channels completely.

GLAZIER'S POINT

## 2. Securing the glass.

◆ Press the pane of glass firmly into the glazing compound.

◆ Fasten the pane securely in place with glazier's points pushed into the frame with a putty knife. Use two points on each edge for a frame up to 10 inches square or one point every 4 inches for a larger frame.

DUCT TAPE

### TRICKS OF THE TRADE

### A Handle to Carry Glass

A handy way to maneuver a small pane of glass is with a handle of duct tape as shown. Use two handles on a larger pane. Make sure the glass is clean and dry before sticking on the duct tape. Gum from the tape can be cleaned off with lighter fluid.

## 3. Beveling the glazing compound.

◆ Press additional strips of glazing compound around the frame so the glass is sandwiched between two beads of compound.

◆ With a putty knife, smooth the strips into a neat bevel that runs from the face of a sash or a muntin (sash divider) to the glass. As you work, dip the knife in water periodically—or paint thinner if the compound is solvent-based—to prevent the knife from sticking. A glazier's knife (photograph) has an end designed for removing old compound, driving in glazier's points, and applying new putty. The V-blade end serves to smooth and bevel the putty.

◆ When the compound has hardened—in five to seven days—paint it to match the frame, extending the coat of paint $\frac{1}{16}$ inch onto the glass for a weathertight seal.

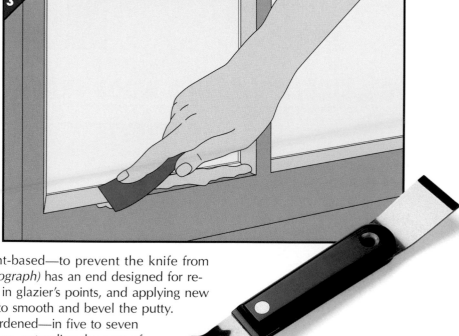

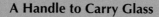

# WORKING WITH A STEEL SASH

## Spring clips.

Some steel windows have flexible V-shaped metal clips to secure the glass, instead of glazier's points.

◆ Remove the old glass and glazing compound as described on page 49.

◆ Pull out the spring clips that secure the glass by pinching them with long-nose pliers *(right)*.

◆ Paint the empty channel.

◆ When the paint has dried, lay a thin bead of glazing compound in the channel, then press the new pane firmly into the compound and replace the spring clips.

◆ Seal the pane with a bevel of glazing compound *(opposite, Step 3)*.

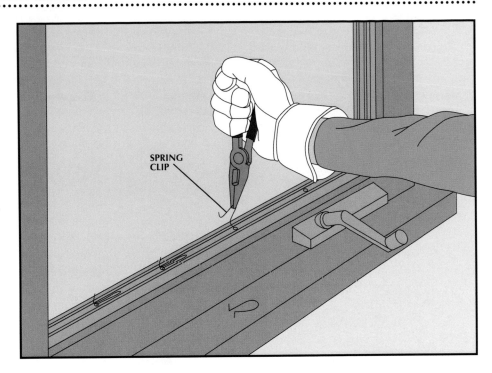

SPRING CLIP

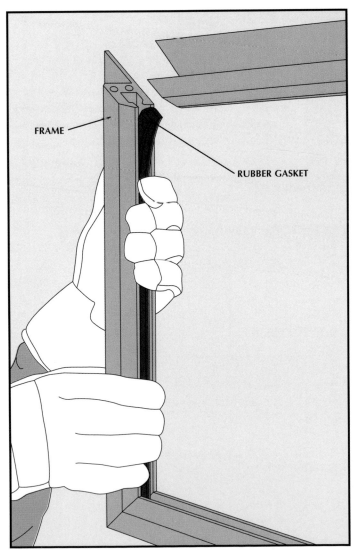

FRAME

RUBBER GASKET

## Rubber gaskets.

In some steel windows, the glass rests in four rubber gaskets, U-shaped in cross section, and the sash comes apart for removal of the gaskets and glass. The model shown has screws at the top and bottom of one vertical edge of the sash.

◆ Remove the sash, unfasten the screws, and pull the side piece from the rest of the frame.

◆ Free the old glass from the gaskets, removing any fragments with a wire brush, and pull the gaskets out of their channels. Replace the gaskets if they are badly damaged.

◆ Fit the gaskets on the new pane, slide the pane into the frame, and refasten the side piece.

In another popular model, the gaskets are sandwiched between the halves of a split sash, and the retaining screws are at the corners of the sash face. With such windows, take out the sash, remove the screws, and pull the inner half of the sash away to get at the gaskets and glass.

# NEW INSULATING GLASS IN A WOOD FRAME

## 1. Removing the old glass.
Most insulating units are held in wood frames by a wood molding nailed in place. For those with a snap-on molding, replace the glass in the same way as for an aluminum or vinyl window *(below)*.

◆ Put an X of duct tape on the broken pane to hold it together.

◆ Determine which side of the window the molding is on by looking for nail holes and seams in the paint. Slip a utility knife between the molding and the window to cut the sealant *(right)*.

◆ Pry the molding free with a stiff-bladed putty knife.

◆ If the seal around the edge continues to hold the pieces together, lift out the glass as a unit. Otherwise, remove the broken pieces carefully *(page 48)*, then pull the edges of the glass unit from the frame.

In some cases, the frame must be disassembled to reglaze the window; remove the sash and look for screws or clips holding the corners of the sash together.

## 2. Putting in the new glass.
◆ Scrape old sealant from the sash and molding.

◆ Run a bead of silicone caulk around the channel and place the new insulating glass unit in the sash.

◆ Nail the molding to the sash, using $1\frac{1}{4}$-inch galvanized finishing nails spaced 8 to 10 inches apart and making sure they do not touch the glass.

# INSULATING GLASS IN AN ALUMINUM OR VINYL WINDOW

## Snap-out plastic moldings.
Insulated glass is commonly secured in aluminum and vinyl windows by four beveled moldings *(inset)* that snap into channels in the frame on the inside or outside of the window. If the moldings show even slight damage, install replacements, available at window dealers.

◆ Put an X of duct tape on the glass.

◆ Cut the sealant between the glass and frame on the side of the window opposite the molding.

◆ Loosen the end of one piece of molding with the tip of a putty

knife; pull the strip from the channel with your hands. Pull off the other strips in the same way.

◆ Remove the glass as described above *(Step 1)*.

◆ Squeeze a bead of clear silicone caulk inside the frame and set the new pane in place.

◆ Push the beveled sides of the two short moldings into their channels one at a time with your fingers *(right)*; fit the long strips last.

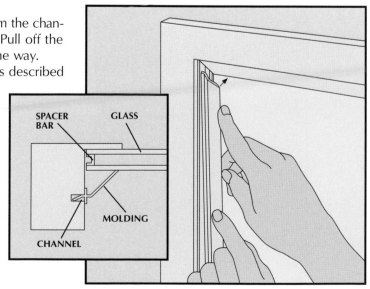

SPACER BAR
GLASS
MOLDING
CHANNEL

# Replacing a Glass Block

Glass blocks are an elegant cross between masonry and glass walls. They transmit almost as much light— usually diffused for privacy—as glass, but they insulate better and offer some of the strength of masonry.

If a block is broken, finding a replacement is usually easy: the standard sizes and designs have changed little since blocks were first popular, and a dealer (usually listed in the Yellow Pages under "Glass Block, Structural") should be able to match your blocks.

Glass blocks are generally held in position with mortar. To make new mortar, mix 1 part portland cement, 1 part lime, and 4 parts masonry sand.

 **TOOLS**

Hammer
Stiff-bladed
  putty knife

Cold chisel
Mason's trowel
Jointing tool

 **MATERIALS**

Mortar ingredients:
  portland cement,
  lime, masonry sand
Pencils or dowels

**SAFETY TIPS**

*When breaking glass blocks, protect your eyes and hands with goggles and work gloves. Also, wear work gloves to protect your skin when working with wet or dry mortar.*

## 1. Knocking out the broken block.
◆ Tape heavy cloth over both sides of the damaged block.
◆ Wearing goggles and work gloves, hammer one side of the block, working from the center toward the edges. Do the same on the other side.
◆ Remove the cloth and sweep out the broken glass.
◆ With a stiff-bladed putty knife, pry off any pieces of glass stuck to the mortar, then carefully remove the mortar with a hammer and cold chisel; take care not to damage the surrounding blocks.

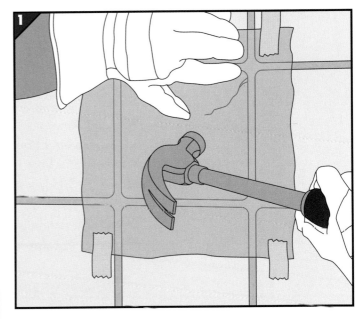

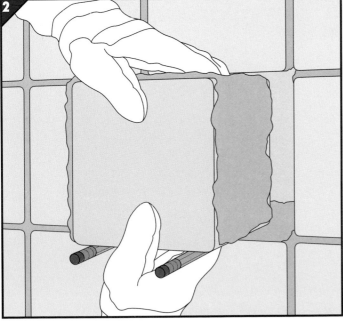

## 2. Mortaring the new block.
◆ With a mason's trowel, spread a $\frac{1}{4}$-inch layer of mortar on the top and sides of the new block and on the bottom of the cavity.
◆ Lay two pencils or dowels in the mortar bed to support the new block and then slide the block into position on top of the pencils.
◆ Pack additional mortar into the joints if necessary and allow the mortar to set for about an hour.
◆ Remove the pencils, fill the holes left in the mortar, and shape concave joints with a thin rod or a jointing tool.
◆ Clean off any excess mortar with a wet cloth.

# Openings for Doors and Windows

Breaking a large hole in a wall for a new window or door may seem like a daunting task. Actually, the process is relatively straightforward. First you need to create and support an opening in the wood framework behind your walls. The method depends on the size of the opening and the type of construction of your house. Then you can cut through the exterior siding or smash through the brick veneer.

Shoring studs with a whaler →

**B**efore installing a door or window, determine whether your house has platform or balloon framing *(below)*. This will affect the rough frame and any additional reinforcements you need to build. The following pages deal with a wide opening and rough frame for a door or window in an exterior bearing wall for both types of construction; framing techniques are the same for nonbearing walls.

**Bearing and Nonbearing Walls:** Walls that run perpendicular to joists, supporting them and resting directly on one another and on girders or solid walls below, are bearing walls.

Exterior walls parallel to the joists do not support them, but require reinforcement if the opening will be wider than 3 feet; use a whaler *(page 65)* as for a bearing wall in balloon framing.

**Simplifying the Job:** Save labor in a framing job by locating the edge of an opening at an existing stud. Also, trace the routes of the cables, pipes, and ducts inside the wall you are opening so as to avoid them.

In some framing designs, a load can be concentrated at one point in a wall; if you find steel columns, wooden posts, or diagonal bracing inside a wall, it is advisable to get an architect

or structural engineer to determine the header size you need. Also consult an expert if an opening in an exterior wall is within 4 feet of the corner of the house.

**Starting Work:** The first task is to remove the wallboard. To avoid a wallboard seam that may interfere with the door trim, cut the wallboard back to the first stud at least 1 foot away from the future opening.

⚠️ **CAUTION** *Before you begin cutting through the wall, turn off electrical power in the vicinity.*

## THE BASIC HOUSES: PLATFORM AND BALLOON

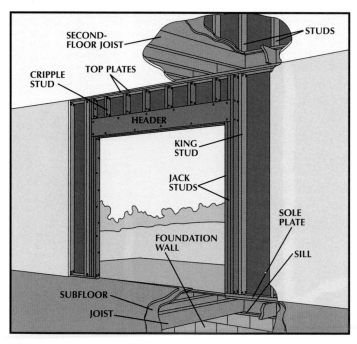

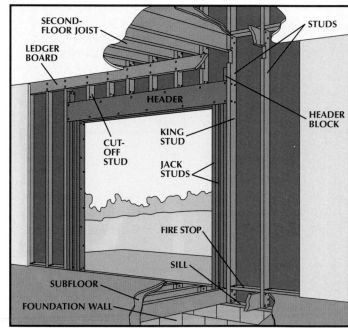

### Platform framing.
A header bridges the top of the door opening. At each side, a full-length king stud is toenailed to the sole and top plates and nailed to the ends of the header. Short jack studs carry the load from the ends of the header to the sole plate. Cripple studs inserted beneath the top plate transmit the weight of the roof and second floor down to the header.

### Balloon framing.
This type of framing has studs rising beside the joists in the basement or crawl space. Because the studs are so long, you cannot insert new king studs; the nearest existing stud on each side of the opening serves as a king stud. The extra-long header is supported by jack studs with additional jack studs at the edges of the opening. The jack studs rest on floor joists or run past them to the sill plate. The studs in the opening are cut to fit the top of the header, replacing cripple studs.

**TOOLS**

Tape measure
Combination
  square
Plumb bob
Carpenter's level
Chalk line
Straightedge
Hammer

Mallet
Wood chisel
Pry bar
Carpenter's nippers
Wrench
Handsaw
Circular saw
1x4 saw guide
Reciprocating saw
Electric drill

 **MATERIALS**

1x4s
Stock for sill
2x4s
2x8s
2-by stock or LVL
  for header

4x4s
4x6
Common nails
  ($2\frac{1}{2}$", 3", $3\frac{1}{2}$")
Lag screws ($\frac{3}{8}$")
  and washers
Shims

 **SAFETY TIPS**

*Protect your eyes with goggles while hammering or sawing. When cutting stucco, you will also need a dust mask; when pulling down wallboard, don gloves and a hard hat. If you are working above the first story, set up scaffolding as a work platform.*

## WOOD AND LVL HEADERS

The most common header, cheaper than a solid-wood beam and at least as strong, is a wood one made by sandwiching two 2-bys around a piece of $\frac{1}{2}$-inch plywood. For all exterior walls and any interior bearing walls, determine the width of the header using the chart found below. For any interior nonbearing walls, build the sandwich from 2-by-4s if the opening is less than 6 feet wide, and 2-by-6s if it is wider. Fasten the boards and plywood together from each side with staggered $3\frac{1}{2}$-inch common nails every 10 inches.

Although it is more expensive, laminated veneer lumber has largely replaced ordinary lumber for use in headers because it offers the same strength in smaller sizes. Nail two pieces of $1\frac{3}{4}$-inch-thick LVL together in the same way as for a wood header, but do not sandwich them around a piece of plywood. To determine the width that is best for your situation, tell the dealer the width of the opening, whether the wall is a bearing wall, and what floor it is on.

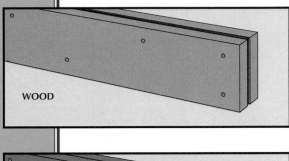

WOOD

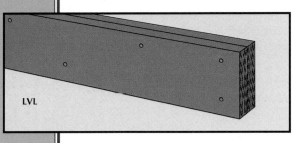

LVL

## Choosing the right header.

This chart can be used to calculate the size of headers made of ordinary lumber. To find the dimensions of the boards, match the span of the opening with the load above the opening; for a span between those listed, use the column for the next larger span. If the space for your span and load is blank, use a laminated veneer lumber (LVL) header. For sizes of LVL headers, consult your lumber dealer.

### Matching a Header to Load and Span

| Load above opening | Span 4' | 6' | 8' | 10' | 12' |
|---|---|---|---|---|---|
| Roof only | 2x4 | 2x6 | 2x8 | 2x10 | 2x12 |
| One story | 2x6 | 2x8 | 2x10 | 2x12 | — |
| Two stories | 2x10 | 2x10 | 2x12 | — | — |

## ⚠ CAUTION

### Asbestos

*Asbestos was once commonly used in wallboard, joint compound, and insulation. It poses a serious hazard when released into the air. If your house was built before the mid-seventies, have the wall material tested by removing a small amount and sending it to a local lab certified by the National Bureau of Standards and Technology. If you suspect your wall materials may contain asbestos, take the same precautions as when removing materials containing lead (page 10).*

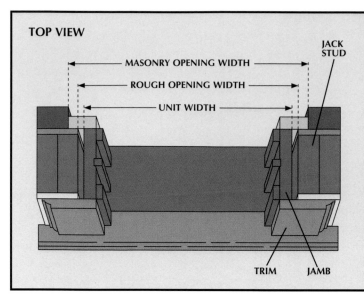

TOP VIEW

JACK STUD

MASONRY OPENING WIDTH
ROUGH OPENING WIDTH
UNIT WIDTH

TRIM   JAMB

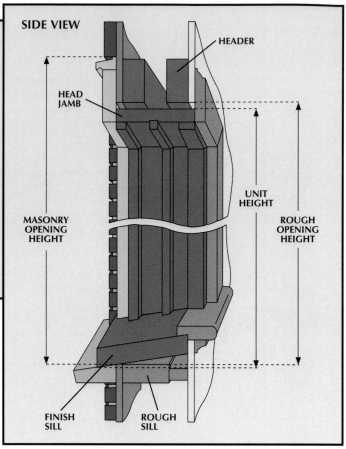

SIDE VIEW

HEADER

HEAD JAMB

UNIT HEIGHT

MASONRY OPENING HEIGHT

ROUGH OPENING HEIGHT

FINISH SILL   ROUGH SILL

## Anatomy of a window frame.

The views of the window opening above and at right indicate the relationships between the dimensions of the unit, the rough opening, and, in case you have a brick exterior, the masonry opening. Once you have determined the desired height and width of the unit, the manufacturer's specification sheet *(below)* will define the size of the rough opening.

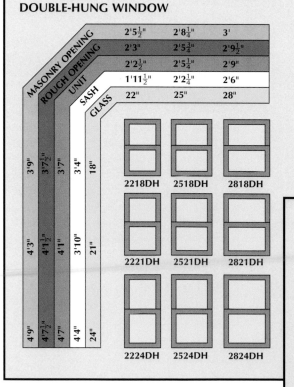

DOUBLE-HUNG WINDOW

MASONRY OPENING / ROUGH OPENING / UNIT / SASH / GLASS

| | $2'5\frac{1}{2}"$ | $2'8\frac{1}{4}"$ | 3' |
| | $2'3"$ | $2'5\frac{3}{4}"$ | $2'9\frac{1}{2}"$ |
| | $2'2\frac{1}{2}"$ | $2'5\frac{1}{4}"$ | $2'9"$ |
| | $1'11\frac{1}{2}"$ | $2'2\frac{1}{4}"$ | $2'6"$ |
| | 22" | 25" | 28" |

| $3'9"$ / $3'7\frac{1}{2}"$ / $3'7"$ / $3'4"$ / 18" | 2218DH | 2518DH | 2818DH |
| $4'3"$ / $4'1\frac{1}{2}"$ / $4'1"$ / $3'10"$ / 21" | 2221DH | 2521DH | 2821DH |
| $4'9"$ / $4'7\frac{1}{2}"$ / $4'7"$ / $4'4"$ / 24" | 2224DH | 2524DH | 2824DH |

## Reading a specification sheet.

Shown at left and below are typical specification sheets for a double-hung window and an exterior door. Numbers across the top indicate the width of the unit and the openings needed for it; those down the side indicate the height. Diagrams in the center represent the unit type, with its order number.

Choose a window based on the unit width and height *(anatomy)*. Build the rough or masonry opening, both larger than the unit to accommodate shims, to the dimensions in the specification sheet. A window with a rough opening that fits neatly between studs minimizes your framing job. Similarly, a masonry opening that is an exact multiple of brick lengths plus mortar joints reduces the number of bricks to be cut.

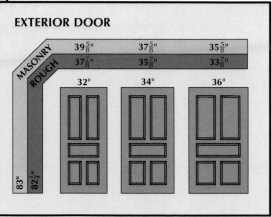

EXTERIOR DOOR

MASONRY / ROUGH

| | $39\frac{5}{8}"$ | $37\frac{5}{8}"$ | $35\frac{5}{8}"$ |
| | $37\frac{7}{8}"$ | $35\frac{7}{8}"$ | $33\frac{7}{8}"$ |
| | 32" | 34" | 36" |

83" / $82\frac{1}{4}"$

# FRAMING FOR A DOOR IN A PLATFORM WALL

## 1. Supporting the load.

Before framing the opening, erect a temporary support structure parallel to the planned opening and about 4 feet from the wall.

◆ To make the sole and top plates, cut four 2-by-4s 4 feet longer than the width of the new door or window.

◆ Mark two of the boards for 2-by-4 studs at 16-inch intervals.

◆ Nail a double 2-by-4 sole plate to the floor, with one of the marked boards on top; use 3-inch common nails to fasten each board.

◆ Cut studs $6\frac{1}{4}$ inches shorter than the distance between the floor and ceiling, nail them to the marked top plate and nail the remaining 2-by-4 to the plate.

◆ With a helper, set the structure on the sole plate and use a carpenter's level to plumb the end studs in both directions. Toenail the studs to the bottom plate.

◆ Attach a 1-by-4 brace diagonally across the partition, from the floor to the ceiling, nailing it to each stud with $2\frac{1}{2}$-inch common nails.

◆ Drive shims between the double top plate and the ceiling at ceiling joist locations, shimming until the structure fits tightly and immovably *(right)*. Recheck for plumb as you work.

If your house has a basement or crawl space beneath the temporary wall, support the floor joists with a horizontal 4-by-6 beam buttressed by 4-by-4 posts. If you are cutting an opening in a second-story wall, erect a supporting framework on the first floor as well as the second.

DOUBLE TOP PLATE

SHIMS

DOUBLE SOLE PLATE

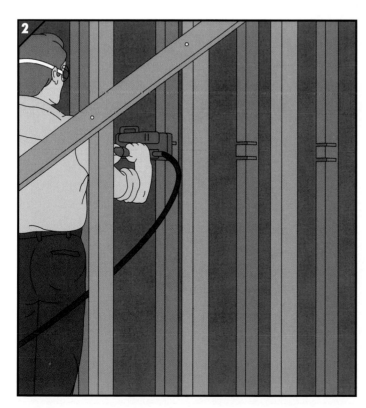

## 2. Removing the studs.

◆ With a circular saw, make two cuts a few inches apart through the middle of each stud within the planned opening *(left)*.

◆ Knock out the small pieces and complete the cuts with a wood chisel. (To saw all the way through the studs at once, cut with a reciprocating saw).

◆ Pry the studs away from the sheathing with a pry bar and remove them.

◆ Cut nails that protrude from the top and bottom plates and the sheathing with carpenter's nippers.

## 3. Laying out the framework.

◆ On the sole plate, mark the center and width of the rough opening *(below)*. Extend the lines across the sole plate with a combination square.

◆ Mark the sole plate 1½ and 3 inches beyond the rough opening lines for the jack and king studs. An opening wider than 6 feet requires a double jack stud; make additional marks 4½ inches beyond the rough opening lines for the king stud *(inset)*.

◆ Drop a plumb bob from the top plate to the king-stud lines and draw matching lines across the top plate.

◆ Toenail 2-by-4 king studs between the plates with 3½-inch common nails.

EDGE OF ROUGH OPENING

EXISTING STUD

JACK-STUD LOCATIONS

KING-STUD LOCATION

## 4. Putting in jack studs.

◆ Consult the manufacturer's specification sheet for the height of the rough opening. Measure this distance from the subfloor and mark each king stud *(right)*.

◆ Cut 2-by-4 jack studs to fit between the mark on each king stud and the sole plate. If you are using double jack studs, nail a jack stud to each king stud with 3-inch common nails, then nail a second jack stud to the first.

◆ Toenail the jack studs to the sole plate with 3½-inch common nails.

KING STUD

## 5. Installing the header.
◆ Make a header appropriate for the size of the opening *(page 59)*. If the header will reach almost to the top plate, consider making it wider to avoid having to install cripple studs.
◆ With a helper, fit the header snugly between the king studs, resting it on the jack studs *(above)*.
◆ Nail through the king studs into the ends of the header; toenail through the jack studs into the bottom of the header.

## 6. Adding cripple studs.
◆ If there is a gap between the header and the top plate of the wall, cut 2-by-4 cripple studs to fit.
◆ Nail a cripple stud to each king stud, set additional cripples in place of the studs you removed, and toenail them to the top plate and the header *(above)*.

# FRAMING A WINDOW OPENING

**Adding a sill.**

A window opening is framed much like a door opening, except that lengths of the existing studs are left in below the sill as cripple studs.

◆ After erecting a temporary support structure *(page 61, Step 1)*, mark the location of the bottom of the header on the king studs the same height above the finish floor as the other windows in the room.

◆ From this point, measure down the height of the rough opening specified by the manufacturer. If the window is less than 40 inches wide, add $1\frac{1}{2}$ inches for a single sill; if it is wider, add 3 inches for a double sill.

◆ With $3\frac{1}{2}$-inch common nails, fasten a 2-by-4 cleat across the studs below where they will be cut, then cut the studs where the bottom of the sill will fall.

◆ After the framing is completed *(Steps 3-6)*, cut extra cripple studs to support the ends of the sill. Nail them to the jack studs and then toenail them to the sole plate.

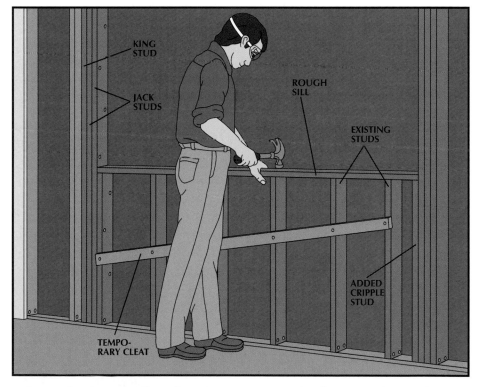

KING STUD

JACK STUDS

ROUGH SILL

EXISTING STUDS

ADDED CRIPPLE STUD

TEMPO- RARY CLEAT

◆ Set a 2-by-4 rough sill on the cripples and toenail it to the jack studs. Nail through the sill into the top of each cripple stud *(above)*. If the open-ing is wider than 40 inches, nail a second horizontal 2-by-4 over the first.
◆ Remove the temporary cleat.

# CUTTING THROUGH THE WALL

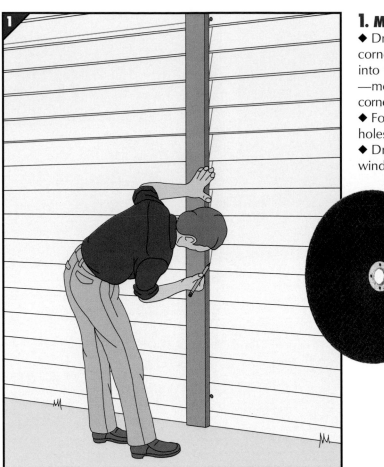

## 1. Making the opening.

◆ Drill guide holes through the sheathing from inside at the corners of the rough frame. (If you have trouble reaching into the corners without tilting the drill, use a long drill bit —more than 5 inches—or drill holes slightly in from the corner and then readjust the marks on the outside.)

◆ For a door, mark the siding $1\frac{1}{2}$ inches below the bottom holes to indicate the bottom of the sole plate.

◆ Draw lines connecting the marks and holes—or for a window just the holes—using the factory edge of a piece of plywood *(left)*.

◆ Cut through the sheathing and siding with a circular saw. If you are working on stucco, use a masonry blade *(photograph)* or an old wood-cutting blade. Special abrasive blades are available for aluminum; a plywood blade can be installed backwards to cut vinyl. To make vertical cuts in overlapping siding, fasten a 1-by-4 to the siding and rest the base plate of the saw on this guide.

◆ For a door, cut through the sole plate along the jack studs and pry out the plate.

## 2. Trimming the siding.

◆ For a window or a sliding door, square the unit with braces as shown on page 74.

◆ With a helper, set the new unit in the opening, butting its brickmold tight against the siding. (In this case, the sliding doors will be installed later.)

◆ Level the threshold or sill with shims, if necessary, and shim the side jambs until they are perfectly plumb.

◆ Trace the corners of the brickmold onto the siding *(right)*.

◆ Remove the unit and connect the marks with a long straightedge.

◆ Set a circular saw to the thickness of the siding. Cut along the outside of the lines to create a $\frac{1}{8}$-inch gap for caulking. Take care not to cut through the sheathing.

◆ Pry away the cut siding.

BRACE

BRICKMOLD

# A DOOR OPENING IN BALLOON FRAMING

LEDGER

WHALER

### 1. Supporting the studs.

To cut an opening in balloon framing, you must build temporary support structures to buttress the floor joists above and below the opening *(page 61)*. You also need to shore up the studs with a whaler—a 2-by-8 about 2 feet longer than the width of the planned opening; this piece will be removed later.

◆ Have helpers hold the whaler against the studs and the ceiling, and nail it to the studs and ledger at each end

with $3\frac{1}{2}$-inch common nails.

◆ Drill pilot holes for lag screws about 2 inches above the bottom of the whaler, into each stud. Install washers and $\frac{3}{8}$-inch, 3-inch-long lag screws *(above)*.

◆ Nail a short plank of 2-by-8 flat on the floor beneath each end of the whaler, then cut a 4-by-4 post to fit between the whaler and each plank.

◆ Plumb the posts, shim them tight against the whaler, and toenail them in place *(inset)*.

KING STUD

### 2. Cutting the studs.

◆ Mark the studs chosen as king studs for both the height of the rough opening and the top of the header.

◆ With a helper, snap a chalk line across the intervening studs at the level of the marks for the top of the header *(left)*. Using a pencil and combination square, extend these lines across the side of the studs.

◆ Cut each stud along the line with a circular saw or a reciprocating saw.

◆ Make an additional cut on each stud within the opening about 6 inches above the floor.

◆ Pry the cut pieces from the sheathing, finishing the cuts if necessary with a wood chisel.

### 3. Nailing header jack studs.

◆ Pry out the fire stop *(page 58)* next to the king stud to make room for the jack stud.

◆ Measure from the marks for the bottom of the header to the joist or sill plate below.

◆ Cut 2-by-4 jack studs to this length and nail one jack stud to each of the king studs with 3-inch common nails *(left)*. For an opening more than 6 feet wide, nail a second jack stud to each of the first ones; if the first jack stud bears on a joist, run the second past it to the sill plate *(inset)*.

◆ Make the header and install it on the jack studs *(page 63, Step 5)*.

◆ Toenail the cut-off studs above the header to the top of the header with $3\frac{1}{2}$-inch nails.

### 4. Adding jack studs at the rough opening.

◆ Mark the width of the rough opening and the positions of the additional jack studs *(page 62, Step 3)*, always doubled in balloon framing, at the sides of the rough opening on the face and bottom edge of the header.

◆ Drop a plumb bob from the header at each mark and draw corresponding lines on the floor *(right)*.

◆ If the additional jack studs are obstructed by the remaining piece of an old stud, cut it and pry out the pieces.

◆ Cut doubled jack studs the same length as those of Step 3; toenail them with $3\frac{1}{2}$-inch nails at the marks on the header and in line with the marks on the flooring. Nail the jack studs to each other with 3-inch nails.

◆ Nail a 2-by-4 as a fire stop between the two sets of jack studs.

◆ Remove the whaler and the temporary supporting structures.

◆ With 3-inch nails, attach a 2-by-4 header block *(page 58)* about 6 inches long vertically to the side of each king stud, directly above the header; this will lock the header in place and keep it from twisting.

## 5. Cutting the opening and adding a sill.

◆ Drill guide holes at the corners of the opening, with the bottom holes at the level of the subfloor. Cut the opening and trim the siding *(page 64, Steps 1 and 2)*.

◆ Knock out all the fire stops within the opening.

◆ Working from the outside, cut the ends of the projecting studs flush with the top of the joists *(right)*.

◆ Extend the subfloor to the outside of the wall with a sill—a board as thick as the subfloor (usually $\frac{3}{4}$ inch), as wide as the studs, and as long as the width of the rough opening. Nail this extension to the joists and to the jack studs at each end with $2\frac{1}{2}$-inch common nails.

# A WINDOW OPENING IN BALLOON FRAMING

WHALER

### Adding a window sill.

For a window, the opening is framed in the same way as for a door, except that the lower sections of the studs are left in place as cripple studs. The fire stops are also left in place.

◆ With the studs supported *(page 65, Step 1)*, mark the king stud for the top and bottom of the header. (The header should be at the same height as the other windows in the room.)

◆ Cut through the studs at the location of the top of the header.

◆ Measure down the height of the opening from the mark for the bottom of the header. Add $1\frac{1}{2}$ inches for a single sill if the window is less than 40 inches wide; for a wider window, add 3 inches for a double sill. Cut the studs at this point *(left)*.

◆ Pry out the studs and install the header *(page 63, Step 5)* and jack studs *(page 66, Step 3)* in the same way as for a door.

◆ Nail an extra cripple stud to the jack stud on each side of the opening with 3-inch common nails.

◆ Nail a single or double sill to the tops of the cripple studs with $3\frac{1}{2}$-inch nails.

◆ Cut the opening and trim the siding *(page 64, Steps 1 and 2)*, then replace the fire stops you removed.

# Breaking Through Masonry Veneer

When making an opening in masonry veneer for a door or window, locate at least one edge along a mortar joint. To avoid cutting lots of bricks, choose a unit from the manufacturer that requires an opening that is an exact multiple of the length of a brick. Otherwise, make the opening slightly larger by extending it to the next available joint. In determining the size of the opening, leave room for the masonry sill *(page 71)*.

The gap between the masonry and the top of the brickmold will be filled with caulk and wooden trim strips. The gaps at the side are filled with brick.

**Special Materials:** Supporting the weight of the masonry requires an L-shaped steel beam, called a lintel, over the opening. Use the table *(right)* to determine the size lintel you need.

Before rebricking around the opening, take a sample of the existing mortar to a masonry supplier who can recommend a mix that will closely match the color and texture of the old mortar.

 **TOOLS**

| | |
|---|---|
| Tape measure | Circular saw with |
| Chalk line | masonry blade |
| Cold chisel | Utility knife |
| 4-pound maul | Scissors |
| 10-pound | Hand stapler |
| sledge- | Screwdriver |
| hammer | Mason's trowel |

 **MATERIALS**

| | |
|---|---|
| Wood screws | Mortar ingredi- |
| (2" No. 10) | ents: portland |
| Angle irons | cement, lime, |
| ($1\frac{1}{2}$" x $1\frac{1}{2}$") | masonry sand |
| $\frac{3}{8}$" tubing | Steel lintel, precut |
| 18-mil plastic | Precast concrete |
| sheeting | sill |

 **SAFETY TIPS**

*When working with bricks and mortar, wear work gloves. Add goggles when mixing mortar or cutting and breaking bricks, and a hard hat if working overhead. If creating dust by mixing mortar or cutting bricks, wear a dust mask.*

| Opening width (feet) | Lintel size (inches) |
|---|---|
| up to 4 | $3\frac{1}{2}$ x $3\frac{1}{2}$ x $\frac{5}{16}$ |
| 5 | $3\frac{1}{2}$ x $3\frac{1}{2}$ x $\frac{5}{16}$ |
| 6 | 4 x $3\frac{1}{2}$ x $\frac{5}{16}$ |
| 7 | 4 x $3\frac{1}{2}$ x $\frac{5}{16}$ |
| 8 | 5 x $3\frac{1}{2}$ x $\frac{5}{16}$ |
| 9 | 5 x $3\frac{1}{2}$ x $\frac{3}{8}$ |
| 10 | 6 x $3\frac{1}{2}$ x $\frac{3}{8}$ |

### Choosing the right lintel.

Use this table to order an L-shaped steel lintel. In the second column, the first figure indicates the height of the lintel's vertical flange; the second, the depth of its horizontal flange; the third, the thickness of the steel. Have the lintel cut to order—16 inches longer than the opening—by a steel-supply house.

## AN OPENING IN BRICK VENEER

### 1. Scoring the opening.

◆ Mark the outline of the opening with a chalk line.
◆ Set a circular saw fitted with a masonry blade *(page 64)* to cut approximately $\frac{1}{2}$ inch deep. Score the horizontal mortar joints between the bricks to be removed at the edges of the opening *(shaded at right)*, working slowly to avoid overheating the saw.
◆ Score the bottom of the opening along a horizontal mortar joint.
◆ Make a similar cut for the top of the opening along a horizontal joint, then score a corresponding line four courses above the top of the opening; these courses will be removed to form the lintel channel.

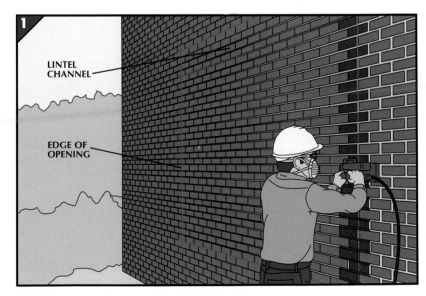

LINTEL CHANNEL

EDGE OF OPENING

## 2. Creating a lintel channel.

◆ At an upper corner of the scored opening, chip through horizontal and vertical mortar joints with a 4-pound maul and a cold chisel. Take out two bricks from the top course of the lintel channel and three bricks from the next two courses. Try not to break the bricks you pull out; you will need some undamaged ones to fill the space above the lintel. If the bricks are difficult to remove, score the horizontal joints within the lintel channel.

◆ At each stud behind the exposed sheathing—here covered with building paper—position a 1½-by-1½-inch angle iron with its upper flange snugly against the brick above it. Attach it to the stud with 2-inch No. 10 wood screws.

◆ Remove three bricks at a time from each of the top three courses and attach angle irons.

## 3. Completing the channel.

◆ Take out the bottom course of bricks from the lintel channel.

◆ Chisel out 8 more inches of brick at each end of the course *(right)* to form supporting surfaces, called shoulders, for the lintel.

### A DRILL AND CHISELER ALL IN ONE

An electric rotary hammer with chiseling capability makes quick work of chipping out mortar between bricks. Although this tool is typically used to drill holes in masonry, it doubles as a miniature jackhammer with a quick flick of a lever near the chuck end of the tool. The side handle gives the user a sturdy grip on the tool.

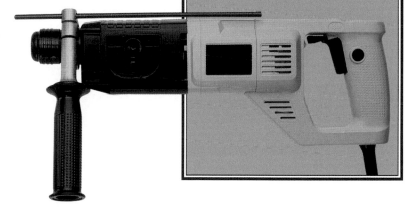

## 4. Completing the opening.

◆ Smash against the center of the opening with a 10-pound sledgehammer to remove most of the bricks.

◆ As you near the edges of the opening, chisel out the remaining bricks one by one in the notched pattern scored in Step 1 *(page 68)*.

◆ Break several bricks in half to make bats, then fill the notched pattern at one side of the opening with these pieces, setting the jagged edges against the sheathing.

◆ Add the amount specified by the manufacturer to the width of your door or window unit. Brick in the other side with bats to create an opening of this width. Unless you have chosen a window that fits exactly, you will have to add partial bricks to every course.

# LINTEL AND SILL WORK

## 1. Setting the lintel.
◆ Apply a bed of mortar to the top of each shoulder so the thickness of the lintel plus the mortar is the same as the existing mortar joints.
◆ With a helper, lift the lintel into its channel, setting the horizontal flange on the shoulders and the vertical flange against the sheathing.

## 2. Stapling the flashing.
◆ Cut a slit in the building paper with a utility knife just above the lintel.
◆ Slip a length of 18-mil plastic under the bottom of the building paper to serve as flashing. Drive staples through the building paper and flashing into the studs between the lintel and the angle irons *(right)*.
◆ Lap the flashing completely over the lintel. Cut the plastic with scissors, leaving $\frac{1}{2}$ inch of the horizontal flange exposed.

When adding a new window to a room, your simplest choice is a prehung unit. These windows come complete with sashes, jambs, and sill, and with the hardware needed to open and lock the sashes. This section will show you how to install a prehung window in a new opening, prepared as shown in Chapter 2. If you are replacing an existing window, you can often change just the sashes. Prehung windows come in all of the four basic window styles: double-hung, casement, awning, and sliding *(pages 8-9)*. Some models are available with tilting sashes for easy cleaning, and handy snap-in screens and storm windows.

**Window Materials:** Your most important decisions in choosing a window are the material the sash is made of and the type of glass. Sashes can be made of wood, aluminum, vinyl, or steel, or wood clad with vinyl or aluminum. Wood is an attractive option and insulates well but is vulnerable to decay and requires repainting; it is also the most expensive material. A low-maintenance and less expensive alternative is vinyl- or aluminum-clad wood. All-aluminum windows are inexpensive but insulate poorly. A bet-ter compromise between cost and energy efficiency are aluminum windows with a thermal break—often a plastic insert that serves as a barrier to heat and cold—or vinyl windows. Both kinds require little maintenance. Steel windows are rarely used today because of their poor insulating properties and susceptibility to corrosion.

Improvements in glazing materials have increased the energy efficiency of windows. Insulating windows have two or three panes instead of one. In some types, the space between the panes is filled with argon gas, increasing the window's insulating properties. Another efficient option is glass with a special low-e—or emissivity—coating. This glass is designed to keep heat in or out, depending on the climate.

**Ordering a Window:** Before deciding on any window unit, note the rough opening sizes required *(page 60)*. When ordering casement or awning units, specify the direction in which the sashes must swing. Once the window is installed add the casing to frame the unit *(see page 29)* and for a double-hung window, a stool and apron *(page 38)*.

**TOOLS**

| | |
|---|---|
| Tape measure | Utility knife |
| Carpenter's square | Putty knife |
| Carpenter's level | Pry bar |
| Clamps | Table saw or |
| Hammer | circular saw |
| Nail set | Jack plane |
| Tin snips | Block plane |
| | Caulking gun |

**MATERIALS**

| | |
|---|---|
| 1x2s | Drip cap or |
| Stock for filler strips | aluminum flashing |
| Stock for jamb | Fiberglass or foam |
| extensions | insulation |
| Shims | Sandpaper (medium |
| Common nails ($2\frac{1}{2}$") | grade) |
| Galvanized finishing | Wood putty |
| nails ($3\frac{1}{4}$", $3\frac{1}{2}$") | Carpenter's glue |
| Roofing nails (1") | Exterior caulk |
| | or spackling |
| | compound |

**SAFETY TIPS**

*Protect your eyes with goggles when nailing or sawing. Drip cap and flashing have sharp edges—handle them with gloves. If you are installing a window on a second story, erect scaffolding.*

# FITTING AND FLASHING

## 1. Squaring the corners.

◆ Set the window unit on a flat surface with the brickmold —or exterior casing—down. Hold a carpenter's square at the corners where the side jambs meet the head jamb or sill. If these corners are not at right angles, clamp one side of the unit to a workbench and push gently against the jamb corners to square it.

◆ With $2\frac{1}{2}$-inch common nails fasten a temporary 1-by-2 brace diagonally between the head jamb and a side jamb; the ends of the brace must not overhang the jambs. Nail another brace between the sill and the jamb on the other side.

◆ Double-check that the window is square by measuring the diagonals: They should be equal.

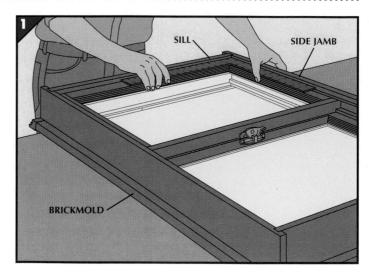

SILL · SIDE JAMB · BRICKMOLD

**2**

BRICKMOLD

SHEATHING

TEMPORARY
BRACE

## 2. Adjusting for wall thickness.

Tilt the window into the rough opening
*(left)* and push it back until the brickmold lies flat against the sheathing.
Inside the house, if the jambs do not
extend past the rough framing enough
to be flush with the wallboard, add
jamb extensions *(page 77, Step 4)*. If
the jambs jut beyond the interior wall
surface, adjust with filler strips:
◆ Push the window out from inside
the house until the jambs align with
the interior wall.
◆ Measure the gap between the back
of the brickmold and the sheathing.
◆ Remove the window from the opening
and cut wood filler strips to the lengths
of the side and head jambs, making
each strip as thick as the gap and as
wide as the back of the brickmold.
◆ Set the strips against the back of the
brickmold and nail them to the jambs
with nails long enough to penetrate
well into the jamb.

## 3. Fitting a drip cap.

For a wall with siding, you will need to
install a drip cap. A brick veneer wall
does not require a drip cap because the
window will be recessed into the brick.
Buy a prefabricated drip cap the same
width as the depth of the brickmold.
◆ With tin snips cut the drip cap to the
length of the head brickmold.
◆ Insert the drip cap between the siding and the sheathing at the top of the
window opening as shown at right.

If you have added filler strips *(Step 2)*,
the drip cap will have to be deep
enough to cover both the brickmold
and the strips. Fashion your own drip
cap from a piece of aluminum flashing, bending the material over a 2x4.

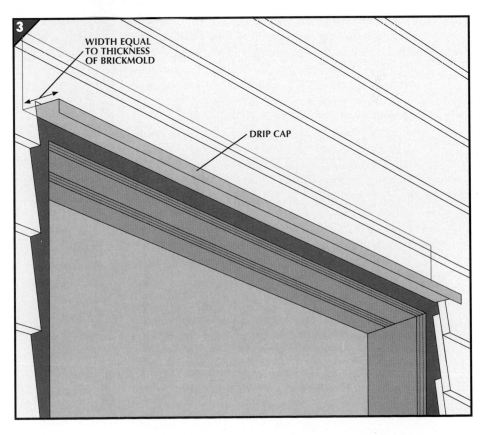

**3**

WIDTH EQUAL
TO THICKNESS
OF BRICKMOLD

DRIP CAP

## 1. Leveling the unit.

◆ Outside the house, center the unit between the jack studs and, with a helper, lift it so the head brickmold fits beneath the drip cap, and the tops of the side jambs butt against the header.

◆ Place a level on the sill to determine which top corner of the window is the lowest. Anchor this corner with a $3\frac{1}{4}$-inch galvanized finishing nail driven through the brickmold into the header.

◆ Lower the other corner to level the head brickmold and nail that corner to the header.

A vinyl, aluminum, or clad window with nailing flanges *(photograph)* is generally attached with 1-inch roofing nails into the sheathing rather than through the jambs—check with the manufacturer.

## 2. Shimming the window.

◆ Inside the house, open the lower sash a crack and check that there is an even gap between the bottom of the sash and the frame; if not, have your helper shift the window slightly from outside so the sash slides straight.

◆ While a helper outside the house holds the window flush against the sheathing, insert shims between the finish sill and the rough sill *(right)*. Always use shims in pairs—insert one with the thick end first, seating it against the brickmold. Cut off part of the thin end of the second shim and insert it thin end first until it is snug. This way, the shims will contact each other and the framing members fully. Shims must fit snugly but not too tightly, otherwise they may push the frame out of square.

◆ Drive $3\frac{1}{2}$-inch finishing nails through the finish sill and the shims below it into the rough sill.

◆ Insert at least two pairs of shims between the side jambs and jack studs on each side of the window frame and nail through them into the jack studs.

◆ Score the shims with a utility knife and break them off.

◆ Fill the gaps between the jambs and studs with fiberglass or foam insulation.

### 3. Securing the brickmold.

◆ Outside the house, remove the temporary braces with a pry bar.

◆ Nail the brickmold to the rough frame every 12 inches with $3\frac{1}{4}$-inch galvanized finishing nails.

◆ Countersink the nails and fill all the holes with wood putty or spackling compound as you would for door trim *(page 32)*.

◆ Wearing gloves, pull the drip cap down tightly against the edge of the head brickmold.

◆ Run a bead of exterior caulk along the joints where the drip cap and side brickmold meet the siding.

For windows with nailing flanges, ask the manufacturer about special brickmolds available to cover the flanges.

### 4. Adjusting the depth of the jambs.

If the jambs of the installed window do not reach the face of the finished wall inside the house and your unit comes with jamb extensions, fasten them in place, then plane their outer edges flush to the face of the wall with a block plane. Otherwise, fashion extensions as follows:

◆ Cut wood strips to the lengths of the jambs and the thickness of the wall material. To rip the strips, use a table saw, or cut them a little thicker than needed with a circular saw and plane them to size.

◆ Leaving a $\frac{1}{8}$-inch reveal *(inset)* to allow for expansion and contraction, fasten the extensions, sawed-side out, with carpenter's glue and nails that penetrate the jambs by $\frac{3}{4}$ inch.

◆ Smooth the rough edges with medium-grade sandpaper.

◆ Run a bead of caulking along the reveal where the jamb and extension meet.

JAMB

$\frac{1}{8}$" REVEAL

EXTENSION

# Handling Windows with Unusual Shapes

Prehung windows are made not only in the conventional rectangular form but in odd shapes designed to fit into limited and unlikely spaces, such as cramped stairwells and shallow attics. These windows generally have fixed sashes. Instructions are given here for the installation of circles, fanlights, ovals, and diamonds, but the directions can be adapted to many other shapes.

**Installation:** Because of their shapes, these windows call for special steps in installation: For example, the opening for a curved window is cut before the rough framing is assembled—the reverse of the conventional sequence. Methods for marking the opening vary from one shape to another. The opening for a circular window can be plotted with a string compass, as shown below, but the straight sides of half or quarter circles must be leveled or plumbed. The shape of an oval window is best traced on a wall from the window frame itself *(page 81, Step 1)*. For curved windows, you will need to cut through both the siding and sheathing together and then put an insert of sheathing back because a saber saw blade cannot be set to cut through the siding only. Circular windows are braced differently from oval ones; windows with straight jambs are braced by yet another system.

**Final Touches:** Finally, add the wallboard and install the interior casing supplied by the manufacturer. If the unit you have chosen does not reach to the surface of the interior wall you will need jamb extensions. Because of the odd shape required, these extensions need to be ordered with the window.

 **TOOLS**

Carpenter's level
Clamps
Nail set
Putty knife
Utility knife
Tin snips

Handsaw
Circular saw
Saber saw
4" saber saw blade
Electric drill
Countersink bit
Block plane
Caulking gun

 **MATERIALS**

2x4s
Exterior plywood
Shims
Flashing
Galvanized common
  nails ($2\frac{1}{2}$", $3\frac{1}{2}$")

Galvanized finishing
  nails ($3\frac{1}{4}$", $3\frac{1}{2}$")
Carpenter's glue
Wood putty
Exterior caulk

 **SAFETY TIPS**

*Wear goggles when hammering or using a power saw, and work gloves when handling flashing. Set up scaffolding to install a window in a second floor wall.*

# PUTTING IN A ROUND WINDOW

## 1. Making the opening.

◆ From inside the house, drill through the sheathing and siding to mark the center of the window.

◆ Outside, center a string compass—a length of string with a nail at one end and a pencil at the other—at the hole and draw a circle to the diameter of the outer edges of the brickmold *(left)*.

◆ Drill a starter hole on the circle and, with a saber saw fitted with a 4-inch blade, cut the circle out of the siding and sheathing. If the sheathing is plywood, save the cutout disk for later use *(page 79, Step 3)*.

◆ Install a rough frame of jack studs, a header, and a rough sill *(pages 58-67)* projecting 1 inch into the cutout opening.

## 2. Installing the braces.

◆ Measure the diameter of the window at the outer edges of the jamb, multiply this measurement by 0.4, then mark and cut four 2-by-4 braces to this length, beveling their ends in from the marks at a 45-degree angle.

◆ Toenail the braces to the jack studs, header, and rough sill with $3\frac{1}{2}$-inch galvanized common nails to form an equal-sided octagon.

## 3. Cutting the sheathing ring.

◆ With a string compass, draw a circle within the cutout disk of sheathing, making the diameter equal to the rough opening required for the window as specified by the manufacturer.

◆ Clamp the disk over the edge of a workbench. Cut out the ring with a saber saw, turning the disk as necessary.

◆ Outside the house, fit the ring into the opening and fasten it to the rough frame and braces with $2\frac{1}{2}$-inch nails.

◆ Caulk the gap between the ring and the sheathing around it with exterior caulk.

If the house has board rather than plywood sheathing, cut the ring from exterior plywood the same thickness as the sheathing.

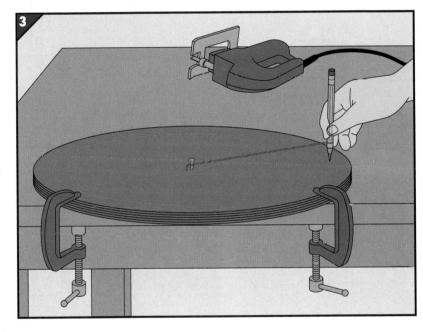

## 4. Flashing the window.

◆ Cut a strip of flashing 4 inches wider than the thickness of the brickmold and as long as half its circumference.

◆ Bend 4 inches of the flashing over the edge of a 2x4 to form a right angle.

◆ Cut tabs at 1-inch intervals in the 4-inch section *(inset).*

◆ Bend the untabbed section around the casing *(left).*

◆ Outside the house, insert the tabbed section of the strip between the siding and the sheathing at the top of the opening.

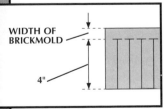

WIDTH OF BRICKMOLD

4"

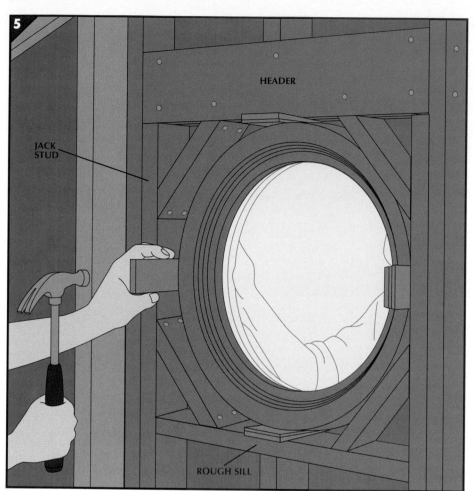

**5. Shimming and
fastening the window.**

◆ Have a helper outside the house hold
the window in the opening, with the
back of the brickmold set firmly against
the sheathing. Inside the house, follow
the shimming techniques described
on page 76 and position eight pairs of
shims between the jamb and the framing parts around it. Shim the rough sill
first, then the header, the jack studs,
and finally the four braces. Nail through
the jamb and shims into the framing
with $3\frac{1}{2}$-inch galvanized finishing nails.

◆ Outside the house, fasten the brickmold to the sheathing and frame with
$3\frac{1}{4}$-inch nails at 8-inch intervals.

◆ Caulk above the window between
the flashing and the siding, and all the
way around the window at the joint
between the brickmold and the siding.

◆ Drive the heads of the finishing nails
into the wood with a nail set, and fill
the holes as you would for door trim
*(page 32).*

◆ Inside the house, score the protruding
ends of the shims and break them off.

**6. Finishing the
window.**

◆ Glue jamb extensions, purchased with the window, to
the edges of the jamb, and
anchor each with finishing
nails that penetrate $\frac{3}{4}$ inch
into the jamb.

◆ After you have installed
the finish-wall material, use
a block plane *(page 23)* to
trim the jamb extensions flush
with the face of the wall.

# FITTING FANLIGHTS AND OVALS

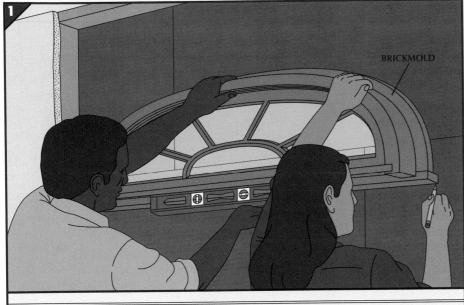

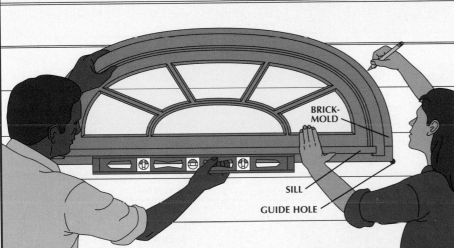

**BRICKMOLD**

**BRICK-MOLD**

**SILL**

**GUIDE HOLE**

### 1. Locating the window.

◆ To expose the sheathing, start the framing procedure *(page 58)*. After supporting the structure, remove the studs, but do not install the header.

◆ Still inside the house, set the brick-mold of the window against the exposed sheathing at the location you have chosen—use a level to be sure the finish sill is horizontal—and mark the bottom corners *(left, top)*.

◆ Set the window down and drill guide holes through the sheathing and siding at the marks.

◆ Working outside, turn the window around to set the brickmold against the siding; use the guide holes to position the window. Recheck the sill to see that it is still level and trace the outline of the brickmold on the siding *(left, bottom)*

◆ Fit a saber saw with a 4-inch blade and cut the traced opening through the siding and sheathing. If the sheathing is plywood, save the cut-out for Step 2.

◆ Complete the framing, with the header, jack studs, and rough sill projecting 1 inch into the cutout opening to provide a nailing surface for the sheathing insert you will make in Step 2.

### 2. Making a sheathing insert.

◆ Center the window, jamb-side down, on the cutout piece of sheathing and trace the outline of the jamb and finish sill. Use the wide edge of a carpenter's pencil so the line will be about $\frac{1}{4}$ inch out from the jamb, which will leave room for shimming.

◆ With a saber saw, cut through the sheathing along the line.

If your house has board sheathing, cut the sheathing insert from exterior plywood the same thickness as the sheathing.

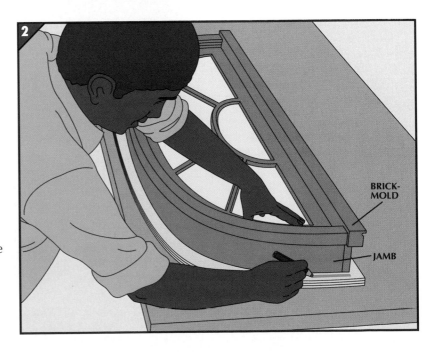

**BRICK-MOLD**

**JAMB**

### 3. Making the braces.

◆ While a helper outside the house holds the window unit against the framing of the opening, work inside to set lengths of 2-by-4 for braces diagonally across the header and the jack studs, $\frac{1}{2}$ inch from the window jamb. Mark both faces of each 2-by-4 at the point where it intersects the header and jack stud; join these points across the edge of the 2-by-4. Remove the window.

◆ Cut the ends of the brace along the marks with a circular saw, finishing with a handsaw.

◆ Toenail the braces to the header and jack studs with $3\frac{1}{2}$-inch common nails.

◆ From outside the house, secure the sheathing insert to the rough framing with $2\frac{1}{2}$-inch galvanized nails, then caulk the joint where it meets the surrounding sheathing.

◆ Flash and install the window unit as you would a circular model *(page 80),* with five sets of shims—two sets under the window and the others at the narrow spaces between the window and the opening.

# SETTING A DIAMOND-SHAPED WINDOW

### Anatomy of a special frame.

The window at right is fastened to diagonal 2-by-4 braces, rather than to the frame. The rough frame *(page 58)* is 1 inch taller and wider than the window; the braces, marked like those in Step 3 *(above),* converge at the midpoint of each side of the rough frame. Each of the four window jambs is shimmed and nailed at two points, and outside the house, the window unit is nailed to the diagonal braces through the brickmold on each side.

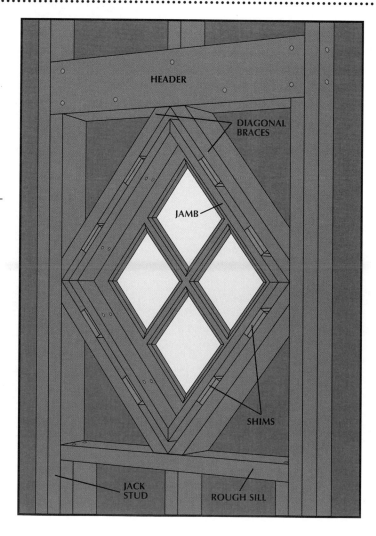

HEADER

DIAGONAL BRACES

JAMB

SHIMS

JACK STUD

ROUGH SILL

**W**ide bay and bow windows are both available prefabricated. Bay windows range from 5 to 9 feet wide in 1-foot increments; most have a fixed center window parallel to the wall and two side windows set at an angle. In a bow window the angle between sections is gentler, forming a graceful curve; this more expensive window comes in 5- to 11-foot widths.

The kits for both bay and bow windows generally include the windows; a head, or ceiling, board; a window seat; and, in many models, an insulating panel below the seat. Some units come with ornamental support brackets called knee braces, which fit beneath the window; for others, you may have to make wooden braces yourself according to the manufacturer's instructions, or have an iron shop fabricate metal ones for you.

**Installation:** Bay and bow windows are installed in much the same way. Prepare the rough opening as you would for an ordinary prehung unit *(Chapter 2)*, but consult the manufacturer's instructions before trimming back the siding from the

sheathing *(page 64, Step 2)*: unlike standard windows, some bay and bow units are designed to rest against the face of the siding rather than on the sheathing. Once the unit is installed, add casing to the inside of the opening *(page 29)*.

**Adding a Roof:** For a window under a roof overhang, cut the opening so the top of the window unit will rest against the soffit when the unit is installed. If the window will have no overhang directly above it, you will need to put on a roof *(pages 86-87)*. In this case, your best choice is to buy a unit that includes a roof kit. Most roof kits do not include shingles or flashing, but once installed, they can be flashed and shingled like any other roof *(page 88)*. Some units can be purchased with prefabricated metal roofs.

 **CAUTION** Do not attempt to install a bay or bow window without helpers to lift the unit into the opening and to steady it on sawhorses.

 **TOOLS**

Long carpenter's level
Long straightedge
Wood chisel
Utility knife
Tin snips
Circular saw
Electric drill
Wrench
Pry bar
Putty knife
Caulking gun

 **MATERIALS**

1x6
Quarter-round molding (1")
Wood shims
Galvanized common nails (2", $2\frac{1}{2}$", $3\frac{1}{2}$")
Finishing nails ($3\frac{1}{2}$")
Galvanized finishing nails ($2\frac{1}{2}$")
Roofing nails ($1\frac{1}{4}$")
Lag screws ($\frac{3}{8}$" x $2\frac{1}{2}$", $\frac{3}{8}$" x 5")
Washers
Galvanized wood screws ($2\frac{1}{2}$" No. 8)
Perforated metal strapping
Fiberglass or foam insulation
Exterior caulk
Metal drip edge
Flashing
Roofing felt
Roof shingles
Roofing cement

**SAFETY TIPS**

*Protect your eyes with goggles when hammering or using a power saw. Wear gloves when handling metal flashing. Scaffolding is a must for installing a bay or bow window on a second story.*

# ATTACHING A BAY WINDOW

### 1. Setting the window in the opening.

◆ With one helper for every 3 feet of window span, lift the unit into place. First rest the bottom of the insulating panel on the sill, then tilt the window up and into the opening so the brickmold butts against the exposed sheathing (or against the siding if recommended by the manufacturer).

◆ Center the unit between the jack studs and support it every 3 feet with sawhorses.

ROUGH SILL

## 2. Leveling the seat board.

◆ Inside the house, find the higher end of the seat with a long carpenter's level and nail that end with $3\frac{1}{2}$-inch finishing nails driven into the rough sill 2 inches from the end jamb.

◆ Shim between the seat and the rough sill until the seat is level. Always use pairs of opposing shims; tap them in lightly with a hammer, taking care not to bow the window frame. At each pair of shims drive two nails through the seat and shims into the rough sill.

Because of their weight, windows 8 feet wide or wider should be shimmed underneath with thin pieces of slate roofing shingle rather than with wood. Nail on each side of the slate.

JACK STUD

END JAMB

## 3. Plumbing the jambs.

◆ Hold a carpenter's level against the edge of each end jamb and have helpers outside the house move the window slightly until the jamb is plumb.

◆ Install pairs of wooden shims 1 foot apart between the end jambs and the jack studs.

◆ Drive nails through the jamb and shims into the stud, taking care to avoid driving a nail through the balancing mechanism of a double-hung window.

## 4. Anchoring the headboard.

◆ Tap in a pair of shims every 8 inches between the headboard and the header. With a long straightedge check for bowing of the jambs; adjust the shims as necessary to straighten them.

◆ Nail through the headboard and shims into the header.
◆ Score all the shims with a utility knife and break them off.
◆ Fill all the gaps between the window unit and the rough frame with fiberglass or foam insulation.

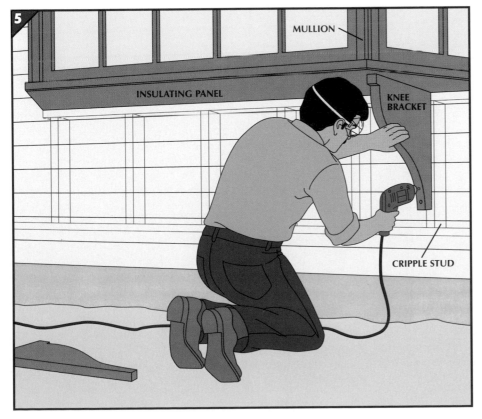

## 5. Fastening the knee brackets.

◆ Outside the house, place a knee bracket—one from the kit or one you made—under each mullion, with the long leg of the bracket against the siding. Drill two pilot holes through the bracket into the cripple stud in the wall. If there is no cripple stud in line with the mullion, toenail one between the sole plate and rough sill.

◆ Fasten the bracket to the stud with $\frac{3}{8}$-inch lag screws, 5 inches long, then secure the short leg to the insulating panel of the unit with a $2\frac{1}{2}$-inch No. 8 galvanized wood screw.

◆ Seal the joints between the window and the siding with exterior caulk.

◆ Nail 1-inch quarter-round molding under the window along the joint between the insulating panel and the siding with $2\frac{1}{2}$-inch galvanized finishing nails.

# ADDING A PRECUT ROOF

DRIP CAP

## 1. Marking the siding.

Roof kits consist of a wooden drip cap, precut end and intermediate rafters, thicker hip rafters, and plywood sheathing cut to fit over the rafters. Some units also include perforated metal straps and fascia boards to cover the end of the rafters.

◆ Nail the wooden drip cap to the trim at the top of the window with 2-inch galvanized common nails.

◆ With a helper, place the three pieces of roof sheathing from the kit against the drip cap and the siding, so the edges of the triangular end pieces overlap the center piece. Mark the outline of the roof on the siding (*left*) and remove the roof sheathing.

◆ Cut the siding along the marks with a circular saw. Set the blade to cut through the siding only. Finish the cuts near the window with a wood chisel.

◆ Pry off the cut pieces of siding.

## 2. Strapping the window to the house.

◆ Fasten a piece of 1-by-6 to the wall studs with $2\frac{1}{2}$-inch nails to serve as a blocking board.

◆ About 10 inches above the top of the window, fasten a length of perforated metal strap to the wall stud nearest each corner of the window, using a $\frac{3}{8}$-inch lag screw $2\frac{1}{2}$ inches long and a washer. (This strap may be included in your roof kit.)

◆ Pull the strap down to the window corner and fasten it to the top of the mullion post with another lag screw. Position the strap so it does not obstruct the hip rafter (*opposite, Step 3*).

MULLION POST

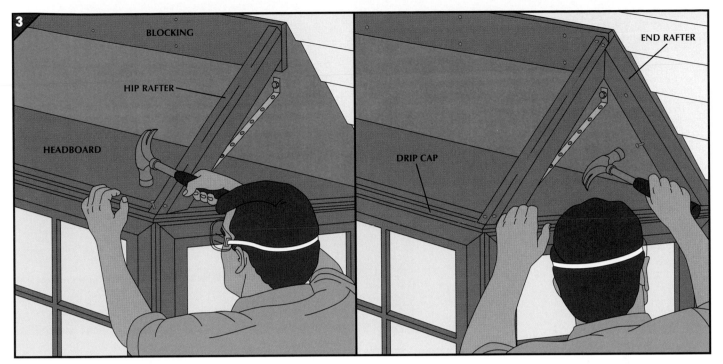

BLOCKING

HIP RAFTER

HEADBOARD

END RAFTER

DRIP CAP

## 3. Installing the rafters.

◆ Attach a hip rafter—thicker than the other rafter pieces in the kit—above each mullion post, placing it so it bridges the gap between the drip cap and the point where the horizontal and diagonal cuts in the house siding meet *(above, left)*. Toenail the rafter to the blocking with $3\frac{1}{2}$-inch galvanized common nails and to the headboard with $2\frac{1}{2}$-inch nails.

◆ At each end of the window, fasten one of the other rafters flat against the wall of the house, nailing it to the headboard, the hip rafter, and the wall sheathing with $3\frac{1}{2}$-inch nails *(above, right)*.

◆ Nail the remaining rafters to the headboard and to the blocking, spacing them at equal intervals between the hip rafters.

## 4. Sheathing the roof.

◆ Place each piece of triangular sheathing over the end rafter and the beveled edge of the hip rafter, then nail it to the headboard and the rafters at 6-inch intervals with $2\frac{1}{2}$-inch nails.

◆ Set batts of fiberglass insulation on the headboard butting up against the triangular pieces. Make sure the vapor barrier faces the warm side of the wall—inside in a cold climate and outside in a hot climate

◆ Place the center piece of sheathing over the hip rafters and the drip cap; nail it to the headboard and rafters at 6-inch intervals.

◆ If your roof kit contains fascia boards to cover the ends of the rafters, place each one tight against the underside of the sheathing and then nail the board to the rafters.

## 5. Weatherproofing the roof.

◆ Nail a preformed metal drip edge tight against the edge of each piece of roof sheathing with $1\frac{1}{4}$-inch roofing nails.

◆ Nail asphalt-impregnated roofing felt over each piece of sheathing and cut away excess felt with a utility knife.

◆ Working from the drip edge up, nail shingles to each face of the roof, trimming them at the hip ridge.

◆ Apply shingles to the hip ridge.

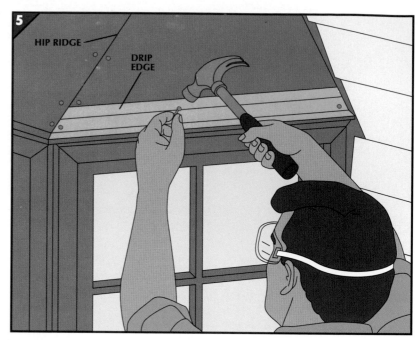

## 6. Flashing the sides.

◆ With a pry bar, lift the pieces of siding just above the roof slightly away from the sheathing.

◆ Working from the bottom of the roof, slip pieces of flashing bent at a right angle beneath each course of shingles and between the sheathing and the siding of the house. Nail the top edge of each piece of flashing to the shingle below it—the next shingle will cover the nail.

◆ Renail the siding.

## 7. Flashing the top.

◆ Bend flashing 8 inches longer than the length of the middle piece of roof sheathing lengthwise into a right angle. Notch the corners with tin snips to fit under the siding at each end.

◆ Slide one edge of the flashing under the siding (right).

◆ Spread roofing cement with a putty knife on the shingles at the roof top and press the lower edge of the flashing into the cement.

◆ Bend the notched projections over the hips and seal all edges with roofing cement.

# A Picture Window

Large picture windows can be custom-manufactured to precise sizes, or you can build your own, as described on the following pages.

**The Glass and Frame:** The size of a large fixed window leads to considerable heat loss in winter—and heat gain in summer—making double-pane insulating glass a good choice. You may want to choose the dimensions of your window to match standard glass sizes. And because such a large, heavy sheet of glass is required, it is best installed by a professional glazier once you have built and installed the frame.

The window frame, which resembles a standard window's but without a movable sash, fits into a standard rough frame (*Chapter 2*). Special lumber with grooves cut in the back to minimize any bowing from expansion and contraction is available for both the sill and the jambs. Sill stock also has edges cut on a slight angle so the sill can be installed on a slope. The lumber is usually either "clear" or made from finger-joint stock (*page 110*).

The glazier will install exterior stops to hold the glass in place (*below*); determine their thickness from the glazier and make your interior stops the same size—at least $\frac{1}{2}$ inch thick for single-pane glass, and $\frac{3}{4}$ inch for insulating glass. Buy brickmold, or exterior casing, wide enough to span the gap between the finish frame and the studs and header of the rough opening; order enough interior casing (*page 29*) for all four sides of the frame.

**Final Considerations:** On a frame for insulating glass, the inside dimensions must be $\frac{1}{2}$ inch greater in height and width than the glass itself, so that the glass can float in the glazing compound; for single-pane installation, allow $\frac{1}{4}$ inch for clearance. And for a good paint seal, both the brickmold and exterior stops should be set $\frac{1}{8}$ inch back from—and not flush with—the jamb edges.

## TOOLS

Tape measure
Combination square
T-bevel
Marking gauge
Clamps
Hammer
Mallet
Wood chisel
Utility knife
Circular saw
1x4 edge guide
Saber saw or handsaw
Paintbrush

## MATERIALS

Jamb stock
Sill stock
Brickmold stock
Stop molding
Interior casing stock
Galvanized common nails ($2\frac{1}{2}$")
Finishing nails ($1\frac{1}{2}$")
Wood preservative

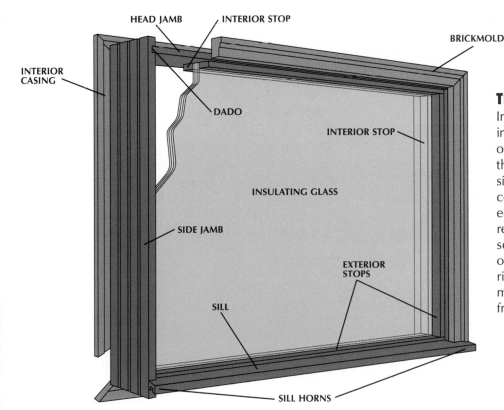

### The parts of a picture window.
In this frame, the head jamb is seated in grooves, called dadoes, at the tops of the side jambs. At the bottom of the jambs, sloping dadoes hold the sill. Strips of brickmold, mitered at the corners, are fastened to the outer edges of the head and side jambs and rest on the horns of the sill. The glass is set against interior stops, then sealed on the outside and secured with exterior stops. After the glass is installed, mitered casing covers the interior of the frame on all four sides.

## 1. Marking dadoes for the head jamb.

◆ One inch from the end of the side jamb stock, mark a line across both jambs with a combination square and a utility knife *(right)*.

◆ Measure the thickness of the head jamb and mark another line that distance from the first line.

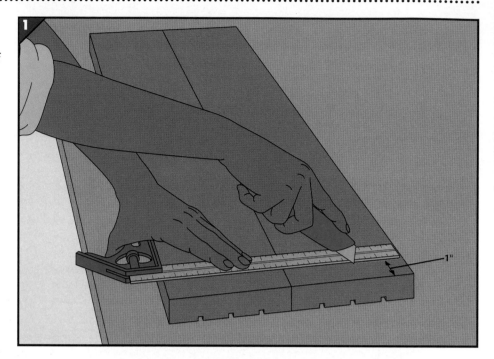

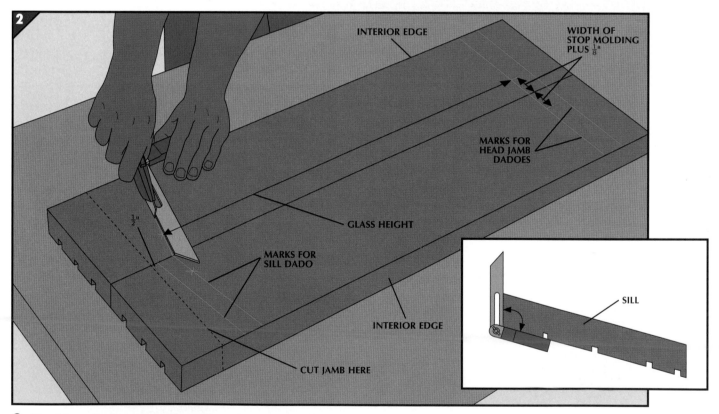

## 2. Marking dadoes for the sill.

◆ Add $\frac{1}{8}$ inch to the width of the exterior stop and mark the line for the bottom of the head jamb dado at this distance from the exterior edge of each side jamb.

◆ From this point on each board, measure a distance equal to the desired height of the glass and mark an X.

◆ Set a T-bevel to the angle of the sill stock *(inset)*, align the blade with each X, and mark one side of a dado for the sill *(above)*. Then mark the other side of the dado to match the thickness of the sill stock.

◆ Cut the jamb stock $\frac{1}{2}$ inch longer than the lowest point of the sill dado.

◆ Set a marking gauge at $\frac{1}{2}$ inch and follow the procedures on page 111 *(Step 2)* to mark the depth of the dadoes.

## 3. Cutting kerfs for the dadoes.

◆ Clamp the side jamb stock to a workbench.

◆ Adjust the circular saw blade to cut to a depth of $\frac{1}{2}$ inch.

◆ Align the blade with the waste side of one of the marked lines. Clamp a 1-by-4 guide to the stock to keep the blade in line, making sure the guide is square to the edge of the stock. Saw along one edge of the dado, holding the base plate of the saw against the guide.

◆ Adjust the guide and cut the other side of the dado.

◆ To remove as much material as possible, saw several kerfs between the first two cuts *(right)*.

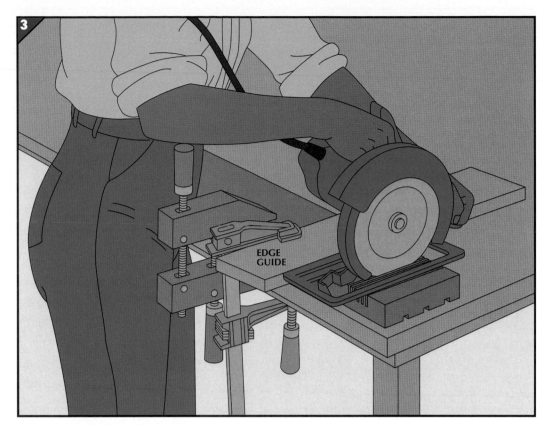

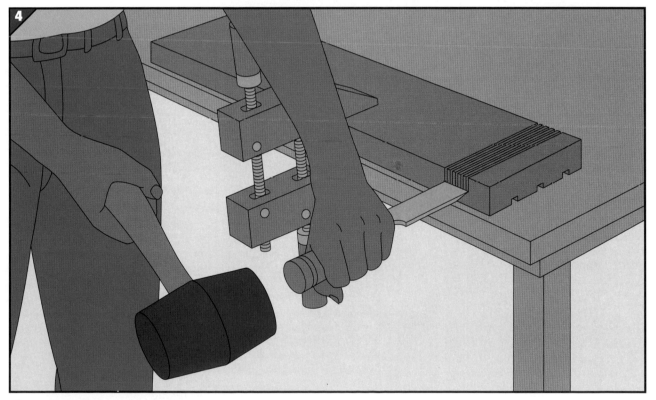

## 4. Chiseling out the dado.

◆ Working from each side of the jamb toward the middle, drive a 1-inch chisel, bevel-side down, into the edge of the jamb just above the bottom of the kerfs *(above)*.

◆ To smooth the bottom of the groove, hold the chisel with its bevel-side up in one hand and guide the blade with the other hand.

The dado cuts required in the window jambs can be made quickly with a router fitted with a straight bit. Fit the tool with a $\frac{5}{8}$- or $\frac{3}{4}$-inch bit and make two side-by-side sets of passes.

Set the bit to cut $\frac{1}{4}$ inch deep. Then, position a guide to align the edge of the bit with the waste side of one of the lines. Make one pass with the router, holding the base plate against the guide. Increase the cutting depth to $\frac{1}{2}$ inch, then make a second pass. Finally, reposition the guide to align the bit with the other line and make another set of passes the same way.

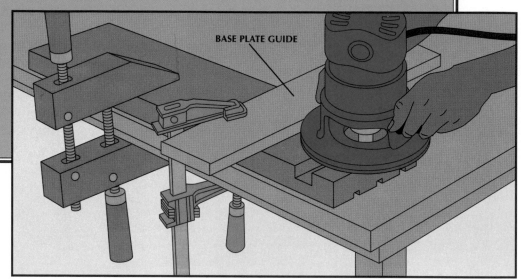

BASE PLATE GUIDE

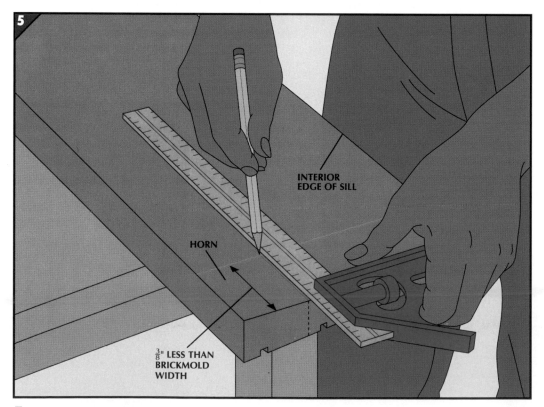

INTERIOR EDGE OF SILL

HORN

$\frac{3}{8}$" LESS THAN BRICKMOLD WIDTH

### 5. Making the sill horns.
◆ Cut the stock for the sill to the inside width of the frame plus 1 inch for the depth of the two dadoes.
◆ Draw a line across the sill at each end $\frac{3}{8}$ inch less than the width of the brickmold.

◆ Along this line, measure from the interior edge of the sill a distance equal to the width of the jamb stock, and draw a perpendicular line to the end of the sill *(above)*.
◆ Cut along the lines with a saber saw or handsaw to form the sill horns.

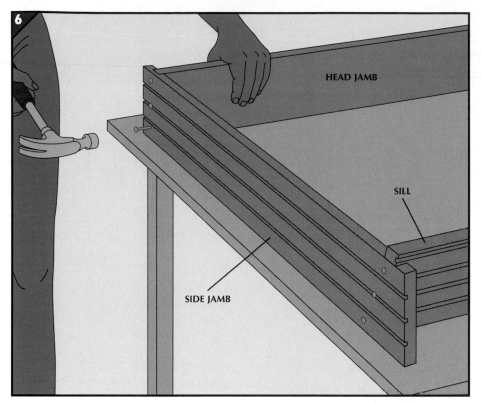

**6. Assembling the pieces.**

◆ Cut the stock for the head jamb to the same length as the sill. Insert the head jamb into the dadoes on the side jambs, then place the sill, exterior-edge up, in the sloping dadoes. Nail the parts together with $2\frac{1}{2}$-inch galvanized common nails, driving them through the side jambs *(left)*.

◆ Turn the frame over and, with the exterior part of the sill projecting beyond the workbench, square and brace the corners of the frame as described on page 74 *(Step 1)*.

◆ Attach the brickmold following the procedure for interior casings *(pages 29-32, Steps 1-7)* with one exception: the bottom edges of the side pieces must be mitered, front to back, at a 15° angle to match the sill slope.

◆ Apply two coats of wood preservative to the frame and nail it into the rough frame, as described on pages 75-77.

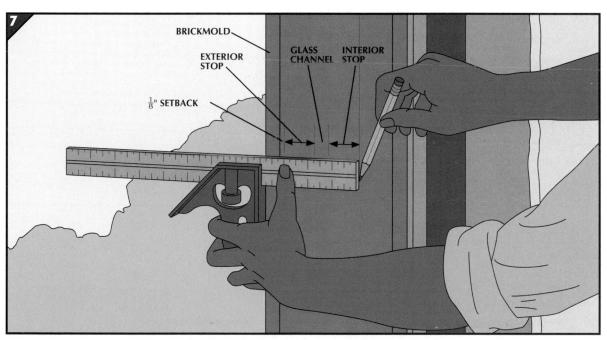

**7. Installing the interior stops.**

◆ Draw lines $\frac{1}{8}$ inch from the exterior edge of the jambs for the setback of the exterior stops, then mark lines for the width of the stop moldings.

◆ Add $\frac{1}{4}$ inch to the thickness of the glass to allow for glazing compound. At this distance from the exterior-stop line, draw a line for the glass channel.

◆ Draw a line the width of the interior stop from the glass channel *(above)* and extend this line onto all four sides of the frame.

◆ Nail the top and bottom interior stops along the line with $1\frac{1}{2}$-inch finishing nails.

◆ Fit the interior side stops between the top and bottom stops: if the interior stops are rectangular, join them with butt joints; if they have a molded surface, cope the joint *(page 33, Steps 2 and 3)*.

◆ Now have the glass installed; the exterior stops will also be installed by the glazier.

◆ Finally, install casings on the interior, as well as a stool and apron *(page 38)*.

# 4

# A Door for Every Purpose

The biggest revolution in doors in recent years is the widespread availability of prehung units, with the frame assembled, the door hinged and mounted, and the lock holes already cut. The entire unit is ready to nail in place. Still, the craftsman's tradition of hanging a door is far from obsolete, and there are occasions when you will welcome knowing how to do the job yourself.

Fitting the latch bolt →

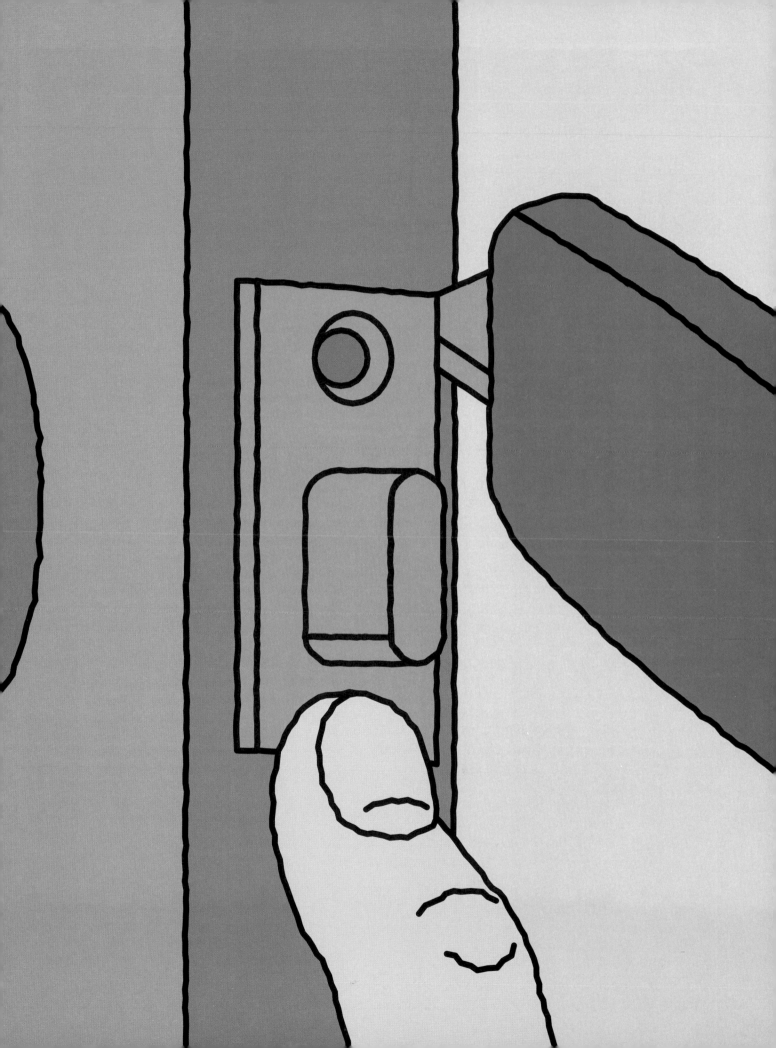

When you buy a prehung door, much of the work is already done. The jambs are fastened together, the door is hinged and mounted, and the lock hole is cut. All you have to do is the final fitting: setting the unit in a rough opening *(Chapter 2)*.

**Exterior and Interior Doors:** Prehung door units for exterior walls *(pages 97-99)* are available with a solid-core wooden door, with a steel-shell door that has an insulating foam core, or a fiberglass door. All types have wooden jambs. These units generally come with weather stripping already installed and an adjustable threshold.

Doors designed for interior walls are either solid-core or hollow-core.

Unlike exterior doors, these units have no brickmold, so you must add casing on both sides of the jamb; the doorstop is a separate piece rather than part of the jamb; and the threshold is often omitted. Still, the installation techniques are similar to those for an exterior door.

Install solid-core doors when noise, security, or the possible spread of fire are concerns. In other situations, you can save money and labor by installing a hollow-core wooden door with a split jamb *(pages 100-101)*. In these units, the casing on both sides is installed at the factory, and the two preassembled jamb sections are slipped into the rough opening from opposite sides to sandwich the wall.

**Double Doors:** Units with a pair of doors *(page 100)* can be purchase for either the exterior or the interior of your home. These doors are hinged in the same fashion as ordinary doors, but they have special hardware and trim. One door is generally kept shut and the other one is active. The inactive door is held at the top and bottom by flush bolts.

**Ordering:** When you order a door from a lumberyard, you must specify the width of the jamb (the thickness of the wall) and the width of the finished door. You must also specify the "handedness" of the door *(opposite)*. For a double door, specify which one will be active.

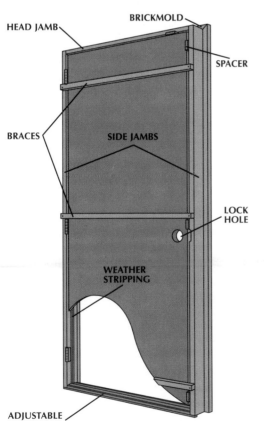

HEAD JAMB
BRICKMOLD
SPACER
BRACES
SIDE JAMBS
LOCK HOLE
WEATHER STRIPPING
ADJUSTABLE THRESHOLD

### Two basic prehung doors.

The exterior door *(left)* comes with weather stripping and an adjustable threshold to seal the bottom of the door. The exterior casing, called brickmold, is already attached; you must add interior casing *(pages 29-32)* after the door is installed. The horizontal braces keep the lock-side jamb from bowing out of square during installation; the cardboard spacers maintain the correct gap between the door and the jamb.

The interior split-jamb door unit *(right)* has two jamb sections that fit together with a tongue-and-groove joint. The casing on both sections is factory-installed.

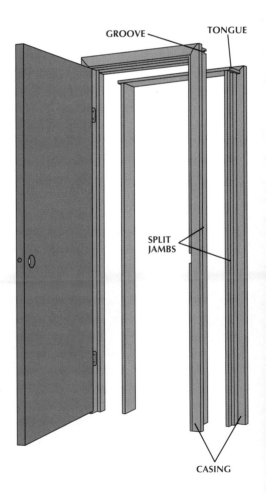

GROOVE
TONGUE
SPLIT JAMBS
CASING

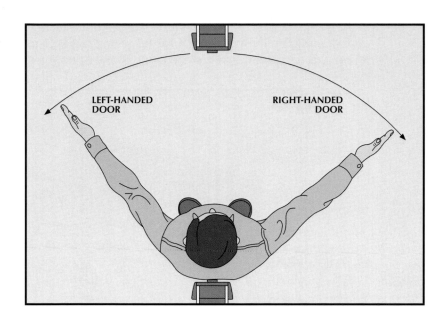

## Left- and right-handed doors.

When you order a door, you have to specify which way you want it to open. This is referred to as the "hand" of the door. To figure out whether you want a left- or right-handed door, stand with your back to the side of the opening where you want the door to be hinged—keeping in mind that the door should open into the room. The arm that reaches in the direction the door needs to open is the hand of the door.

# INSTALLING AN EXTERIOR DOOR

## 1. Preparing the opening.

◆ Apply three parallel beads of exterior caulk along the subfloor where the threshold of the new doorframe will rest and 6 inches up the jack studs at the sides of the opening.

◆ If your door unit is not designed to rest on the subfloor, install the spacer provided by the manufacturer or cut a wooden one from lumber or exterior-grade plywood as thick as the finish floor; make the spacer as wide as the door jambs and long enough to fit the space between the jack studs.

◆ Press the spacer into the caulk, with its outside edge flush with the sheathing, and check it with a carpenter's level. If necessary, shim below the spacer every 8 inches to level it.

◆ Fasten the spacer with $2\frac{1}{2}$-inch galvanized common nails in a staggered pattern.

◆ Apply three more beads of caulk on top of the spacer and a long, zigzag bead of caulk to the face of the sheath-

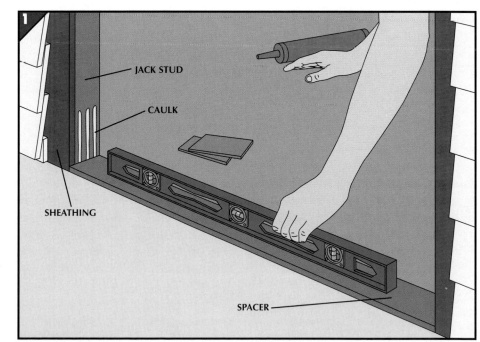

ing around the sides and top of the rough opening.

◆ Install a drip cap at the top of the opening *(page 75, Step 3)*.

If your door unit is designed to sit on the subfloor, level the threshold with shims when you set the door in the opening *(Step 2)*.

## 2. Setting the door in place.

◆ Set the bottom of the unit on the spacer—or on the subfloor if you are not using a spacer. Have a helper outside the house tilt the door upright and hold the brickmold tight against the sheathing. If the jambs protrude past the interior wall surface, add filler strips *(page 75, Step 2)*.

◆ Inside the house, center the unit in the opening and insert pairs of shims between the side jambs and the jack studs at the heights of the hinges. First, insert the butt end of one shim. Trim the thin end of a second shim with a utility knife, insert the cut end, and tap it lightly with a hammer or push it in by hand until it is snug, being careful not to bow the jambs. Do not nail the jambs to the studs yet.

## 3. Plumbing the hinge jamb.

◆ Hold a level against the face of the hinge-side brickmold; pull the jamb out at the top or bottom to plumb the brickmold *(above)*.

◆ Set the level against the inside edge of the brickmold and adjust the shims to plumb the brickmold from left to right.

◆ Drive $3\frac{1}{4}$-inch galvanized finishing nails through the hinge-side brickmold into the framing.

## 4. Squaring the door.

◆ Inside the house, check the gap between the head jamb and the door. If the gap is narrower at the lock side, tighten the shims behind the top hinge and the bottom of the lock-side jamb; if the gap is wider on the lock side, loosen all of the shims slightly and tighten the pairs of shims at the bottom hinge and the top of the lock-side jamb until the gap is even.

◆ Outside the house, nail the lock-side brickmold and the top of the brickmold to the framing.

## 5. Straightening the lock-side jamb.

◆ Check from inside the house whether the top or bottom of the door protrudes beyond the edge of the lock-side jamb; at the same time, have a helper outside check to be sure that the brickmold is tight against the sheathing.

◆ If the bottom of the door protrudes inside, loosen the shims of the lock-side jamb. Hold a block of wood against this jamb near the top and tap the block with a hammer to push the jamb and brickmold outward until the door meets the jamb at both top and bottom. If the top of the door protrudes, push the jamb outward at the bottom.

◆ Check outside to be sure that the door is tight against the stop at both top and bottom; then tighten the pairs of shims at the top and bottom of the lock-side jamb.

## 6. Shimming around the rest of the door.

◆ Adjust the center pair of shims behind the lock-side jamb until the gap between the door and the jamb is even (right).

◆ Insert two pairs of shims between the head jamb and the header, adjusting them until the gap between the door and head jamb is even.

◆ If the door is higher than 6 feet 8 inches or if the gap between the side jamb and door varies on the lock or hinge side, add pairs of shims midway between the hinges on each side, adjusting them until the gap is even.

◆ With a pry bar remove the braces and spacers installed by the manufacturer and open the door.

◆ At each shim location, drive two $3\frac{1}{2}$-inch galvanized finishing nails through the jamb and shims into the jack stud.

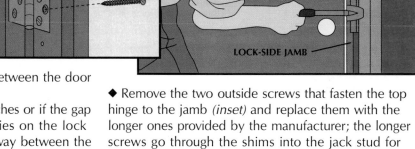

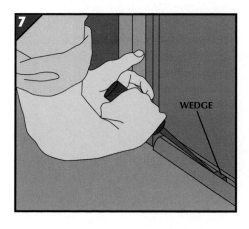
JACK STUD

LOCK-SIDE JAMB

◆ Remove the two outside screws that fasten the top hinge to the jamb (inset) and replace them with the longer ones provided by the manufacturer; the longer screws go through the shims into the jack stud for added support.

◆ Score all the shims with a utility knife and break them off. Trim the edges flush to the jamb with a wood chisel if necessary.

◆ Set all the nails and fill with wood putty or spackling compound.

WEDGE

## 7. Adjusting the sill.

◆ Inside the house, close the door and follow the manufacturer's instructions to raise the threshold until a piece of paper slipped beneath the door just catches on the weather stripping. In the widely used model shown here, the threshold is raised by sliding wedges to the right between the sill and threshold with a screwdriver; other models have adjusting screws. Do not raise the threshold too high—it can damage the vinyl weather stripping.

◆ Fill the space between the jack studs and the side jambs with foam or fiberglass insulation.

◆ Outside, caulk the joint between the brickmold and the siding.

# ALIGNING A SET OF DOUBLE DOORS

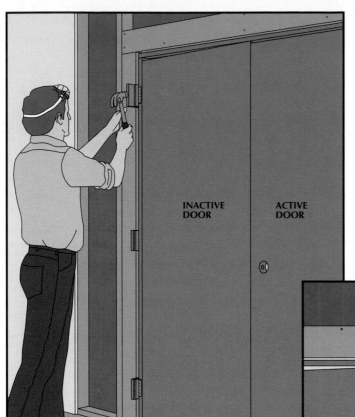

INACTIVE DOOR

ACTIVE DOOR

HEADER

HEAD JAMB

### Squaring the doors.
◆ Center, shim, and plumb the doors *(pages 97 to 98, Steps 1-3)*, treating the jamb for the inactive door as you would the hinge-side jamb of a single door.
◆ Loosen the pairs of shims behind the top and bottom hinges of both doors and check the gap between each door and the head jamb where the doors meet *(inset)*. Tighten the shims behind the top hinge of the higher door until the gap is the same for both doors.
◆ Tighten all the shims, rechecking the gap.
◆ Adjust the active-door jamb as you would the lock-side jamb of a single door *(page 99, Steps 5-6)*.
◆ Insert three sets of shims between the header and the head jamb and adjust them until the gap between the head jamb and the door is even.
◆ Drive two $3\frac{1}{2}$-inch galvanized finishing nails through the jambs and each set of shims into the framing.
◆ Replace the top screws on the top hinge of both doors with the longer ones provided by the manufacturer.

# A SPLIT JAMB FOR INTERIOR DOORS

### 1. Installing the door.
◆ Slide the jamb section containing the door into the rough opening, resting the door on two pairs of shims. Insert pairs of shims behind the side jambs at the heights of the hinges.
◆ Adjust the shims behind the hinge-side jamb until the jamb is plumb *(right)*.
◆ If the gap between the lock-side corner of the head jamb and the door is more than $\frac{1}{8}$ inch, trim the bottom of the lock-side jamb by about $\frac{1}{16}$ inch; leave the door in place and use a flush-cutting saw *(photograph)*.
◆ Nail the hinge-side casing to the wall with $1\frac{1}{2}$-inch finishing nails into the jamb and 2-inch nails into the framing.

SHIMS

## Props for a Level

Holding a long level in place on a door jamb while shimming normally calls for the aid of a helper. Another solution is to wedge the level against the jamb with thin pieces of scrap lumber, as shown at right. Then, simply keep an eye on the level as you adjust the shims.

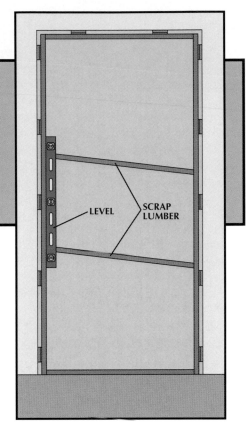

LEVEL    SCRAP LUMBER

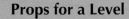

¼" GAUGE

## 2. Adjusting the casing.

◆ With a $\frac{1}{8}$-inch gauge, such as a piece of corrugated cardboard, adjust the top casing until there is a $\frac{1}{8}$-inch gap between the head jamb and the door, then nail the casing to the header with 2-inch finishing nails.

◆ Similarly, adjust the gap between the door and the lock-side jamb and nail the lock-side casing.

◆ From the other side of the door, insert pairs of shims above the head jamb, behind the middle of the hinge-side jamb, and behind the lock-side jamb.

◆ Drive two $3\frac{1}{2}$-inch finishing nails through each pair.

◆ Score the shims with a utility knife and then break them off flush with the edge of the jambs.

CASING

FIRST JAMB SECTION    GROOVE

SECOND JAMB SECTION    TONGUE

## 3. Finishing the jamb installation.

◆ Fit the tongue of the second jamb section into the groove of the first one *(inset)*, then push the second section inward until the attached casing rests against the wallboard.

◆ Fasten the casing as in Step 1 *(opposite)*.

◆ Drive $3\frac{1}{2}$-inch finishing nails through the second jamb section and the shims into the rough framing.

**A**n ordinary lock can be installed with just one tool—a screwdriver. The lock manufacturer provides the hardware and, if you buy the lock before you order a prehung door and give the template and specifications that come with the lock to the door supplier, the necessary holes in the door and jamb can be bored for you. Otherwise, you will have to do the job yourself *(page 118)*.

Door locks and latches come in five main types. A privacy lock *(right)*, commonly used for bedrooms and bathrooms, can be locked from the inside with a push button. Passage latches for interior doors have similar knobs and bolt, but no locking mechanisms. An entrance lock is similar to a privacy lock but it can be locked from both sides—with a key from outside and a push button inside.

Both the passage and entrance lock are installed the same way as a privacy lock. The type with a dead-locking plunger, which locks the bolt when the door is shut, is more difficult to pick. For extra security, add a dead-bolt lock *(opposite)*, which has a heavy bolt that slides into the jamb. A common variation on a dead-bolt is the rim lock, also shown opposite.

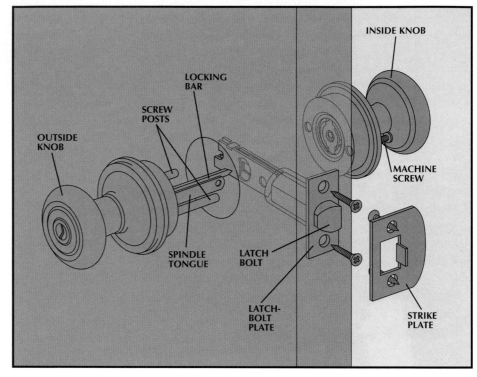

**Installing a privacy lock.**
◆ Position the strike plate over the hole in the jamb and screw it in place.
◆ Slip the latch bolt into its hole in the door, with the beveled side of the bolt facing the strike plate as the door is closed, and screw the latch-bolt plate in place.
◆ Depress the latch bolt about $\frac{1}{8}$ inch

and slip the outside-knob unit into the door, sliding the screw posts, spindle tongue, and the locking bar, through the latch-bolt holes.
◆ Slide the inside-knob unit onto the spindle tongue and locking bar, align its holes with the screw posts, and fasten the knob units together with the machine screws provided with the lock.

## KEYLESS LOCKS

A range of keyless locks is available, putting an end to the headaches of misplaced keys. They include models operated by a pushbutton combination keypad, a magnetic card, or a knob that is rotated like a traditional combination lock. The keypad type shown at right is mechanically operated; there are also electronic models with the strike wired to a control box inside the house.

## A new dead-bolt lock.

◆ Fasten the steel reinforcing plate with 3-inch screws driven through the jamb into the stud, then fasten the decorative strike plate over the steel one.

◆ Turn the tip of a screwdriver in the drive-bar slot of the bolt assembly to extend the bolt, slip the assembly into the door with the slot down, and screw the bolt plate to the door.

◆ Adjust the lock for the thickness of the door: On this model, you can select a trim ring of the correct thickness; on others, you may have to cut off the tip of the drive bar.

◆ Slide the cylinder into the door from outside, slipping the drive bar through the slot in the bolt assembly and aligning the cylinder and assembly holes.

◆ Slide the thumb turn into position over the drive bar and screw it to the cylinder.

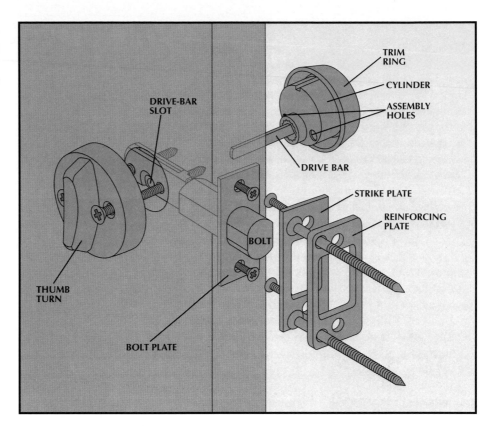

## Adding a rim lock.

◆ Screw the strike plate to the jamb.

◆ Insert the cylinder from the outside, screw the rear reinforcing plate to it, and set the lock case against the door so the drive bar fits into the thumb turn slot of the case. If necessary, shorten the drive bar by snapping it at one of the grooves with pliers.

◆ Secure the lock case in position with screws that penetrate at least 1 inch into the door.

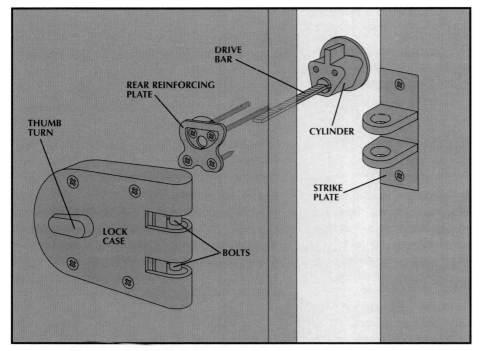

103

# Sliding Doors for Tight Places

Sliding glass doors *(below)*, run on rollers along a track; the pocket door *(page 107)*, a variation of the sliding door, glides into a metal frame that is built into the wall.

**Sliding Doors:** These doors are sold in kits containing the doors, a frame, and all the needed hardware; it should also include flexible weather stripping. Door frames are wood or aluminum. Wooden doors are more expensive, but are more efficient insulators. Better models of aluminum doors have a hollow core filled with foam insulation. The widely used type of wood sliding door shown on these pages has two door panels, one stationary and one movable, but three- and four-panel units are also available. Note that many building codes require almost-shatterproof tempered glass for sliding doors.

Start the installation with a rough opening *(Chapter 2)* $\frac{3}{8}$ inch higher at the top and wider at each side than the door frame; take pains to make the opening plumb and square because the clearances are critical.

**Pocket Doors:** These doors require a steel frame inside the wall including prefabricated steel split jamb and split stud, wooden nailing strips, and over- head track and various hardware *(pages 107-109)*. The models like the one shown on these pages have tracks that telescope to accept doors from 2 to 3 feet wide; other models have fixed tracks, which can be cut down for a door less than 3 feet wide. The door itself, preferably a hollow- core interior door, is bought separate- ly along with the door hardware.

You will have to frame an open- ing wide enough for both the door and the frame. Check the manufac- turer's specifications to determine the exact size of the rough frame. Once the steel frame is installed, it is covered with wallboard.

 **TOOLS**

| | | |
|---|---|---|
| Tape measure | Screwdriver | Backsaw |
| Carpenter's | Wrench | Hacksaw |
| level | Prybar | Table saw |
| Straightedge | Utility | Circular saw |
| Chalk line | knife | and jack |
| Hammer | Miter box | plane |

 **MATERIALS**

| | |
|---|---|
| Stock for sill nosing | Galvanized finishing |
| Stop molding | nails (2", $3\frac{1}{4}$") |
| Jamb stock | Galvanized wood |
| Shims | screws (3" No. 8) |
| Common nails | Drip cap |
| ($2\frac{1}{2}$", $3\frac{1}{2}$") | Exterior caulk |

 **SAFETY TIPS**

*Protect your eyes with goggles when hammering nails.*

# INSTALLING A SLIDING DOOR

## 1. Securing the threshold.
◆ Assemble the frame by fastening the head jamb and threshold to the side jambs with the screws provided.
◆ Square and brace the unit *(page 74),* but fasten the braces to the outside.
◆ Run three parallel beads of caulk along the subfloor where the thresh- old will rest.
◆ Center the frame in the opening from the outside and press down on it to even out the caulk.
◆ While a helper holds the brickmold flush against the sheathing, fasten the interior edge of the threshold to the sill every 12 inches through the predrilled holes with the screws provided.

BRICKMOLD

## 2. Fastening the frame.

◆ Install a drip cap *(page 75, Step 3)* over the head brickmold.
◆ With a level, plumb the brickmold and fasten it to the rough framing with $3\frac{1}{4}$-inch galvanized finishing nails spaced a foot apart.
◆ Tap in shims *(page 98)* behind the predrilled holes in the frame—five pairs between each side jamb and jack stud and three pairs between the head jamb and the header. To be sure you do not bow the jamb, have a helper hold a straightedge against it while you work *(right)*.
◆ Screw the jambs to the jack studs and the header through the predrilled holes. Use the screws provided or 3-inch galvanized No. 8 wood screws.
◆ Remove the braces with a pry bar, then score the protruding ends of the shims with a utility knife and break them off.

**JACK STUD**

**JAMB**

**SHIMS**

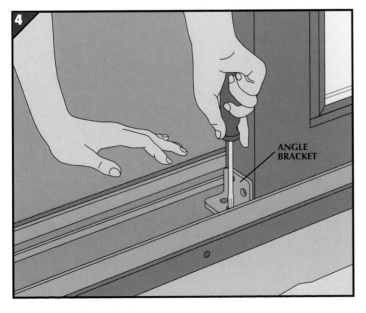

## 3. Supporting the threshold.

◆ Cut a piece of wood to fit under the threshold overhang; rip it with a table saw or cut it slightly thicker than needed with a circular saw and plane it to size.
◆ Position the strip under the threshold and nail it to the sheathing with 2-inch galvanized finishing nails *(above)*.

**ANGLE BRACKET**

## 4. Installing the stationary door panel.

◆ Lift the stationary panel—the one without a latch—into the outside channel of the frame and slide it into the groove in the side jamb. If the panel does not slide all the way into the groove, wedge a length of 2-by-4 at an angle between the panel and the opposite side jamb; press down on the 2-by-4 to push the panel into place.
◆ Screw the top and bottom angle brackets provided by the manufacturer to the threshold *(left)* and the head jamb.

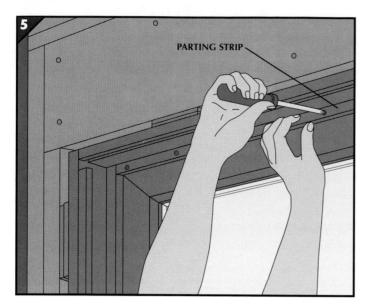

## 5. Fastening the parting strip.

Screw the top parting strip, which separates the stationary and movable panels, into the stationary panel with the screws provided. In the model shown here, the strip is located in a groove along the center of the head jamb. The side parting strips come already installed in the side jambs.

## 6. Installing the movable door panel.

◆ Set the rollers in the inside channel of the frame so the door rides on the raised ridge, then tilt the door into the channel at the top of the frame (right).

◆ Fit the head stop into the shallow groove along the underside of the head jamb so it rests snugly against the weather stripping on the head jamb. Screw the stop to the jamb.

In some models, the head stop is an integral part of the frame. With this type, angle the top of the movable panel into place behind the stop, swing the bottom inward, and ease the panel down until the rollers rest in the channel.

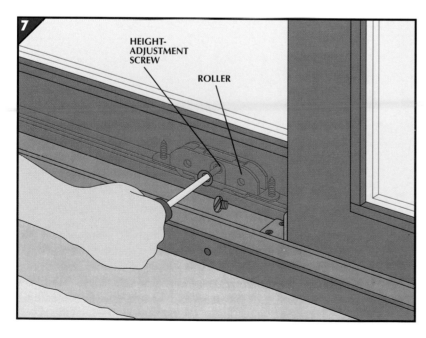

## 7. Plumbing the movable panel.

Close the movable panel. If it is not plumb against the side jamb, adjust the height of one edge of the door.

◆ Pry off the plastic guard caps in the bottom rail.

◆ Turn the height-adjustment screws (left) to raise or lower the door over the rollers until the door meets the side jamb squarely.

◆ Install casing (pages 29-32) on the inside.

# HANGING A POCKET DOOR

## 1. Cutting the nailing strips.

◆ If your unit has a telescoping overhead track, unscrew the wooden nailing strips from the sides of the track.
◆ With a miter box, cut the strips $1\frac{1}{4}$ inches longer than the width of the door.
◆ Loosen the two screws that secure the center bracket of the track. Telescope the track to the width of the opening; slide the bracket to the center of the track and retighten the center-bracket screws.
◆ Reattach the nailing strips *(right)*.

If your model has a fixed overhead track, detach the nailing strips and cut them with a backsaw to the length specified by the manufacturer. Then cut the track with a hacksaw, affix the end brackets provided by the manufacturer, and reattach the nailing strips.

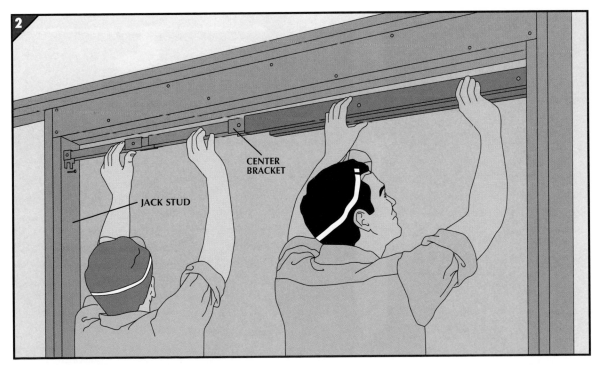

NAILING STRIP

CENTER BRACKET

CENTER BRACKET SCREWS

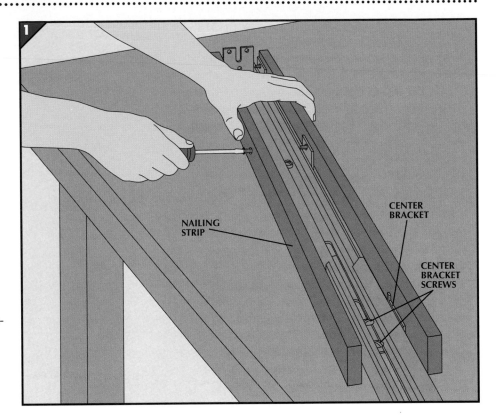

CENTER BRACKET

JACK STUD

## 2. Hanging the overhead track.

◆ Drive $3\frac{1}{2}$-inch common nails partway into the center of the jack studs $1\frac{1}{2}$ inches higher than the final position of the door. With a helper hang the track on the nails *(above)*.
◆ Check the track with a level and have your helper raise the lower end until the track is horizontal.

Drive nails through the holes in the ends of the track into the jack studs to secure the track in place, then remove the temporary nails.
◆ Snap chalk lines on the floor between the jack studs, marking their outside edges so you can locate the bottom positions of the split jamb and split stud later *(page 108, Step 4)*.

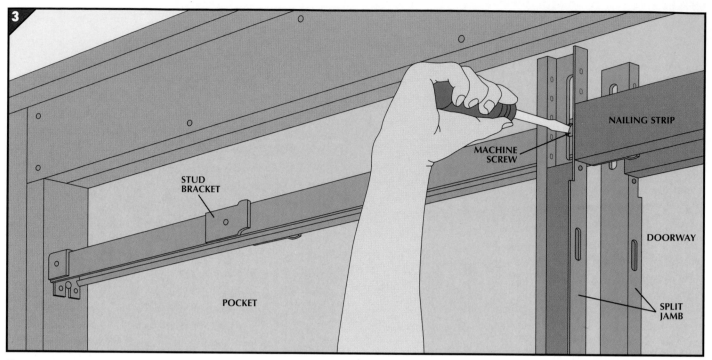

STUD
BRACKET

MACHINE
SCREW

NAILING STRIP

DOORWAY

POCKET

SPLIT
JAMB

### 3. Fastening the split jamb and stud to the track.

◆ Fit the top of the split jamb around the track and rest the jamb on the floor.

◆ Drive the machine screws provided by the manufacturer through the slots of the split jamb top into the holes in the center bracket *(above)*.

◆ Mount the split stud the same way, fastening it to the fixed stud bracket located at the center of the pocket.

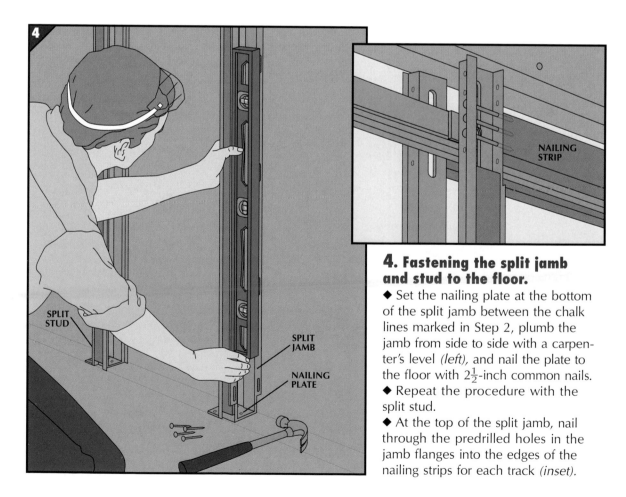

NAILING
STRIP

SPLIT
STUD

SPLIT
JAMB

NAILING
PLATE

### 4. Fastening the split jamb and stud to the floor.

◆ Set the nailing plate at the bottom of the split jamb between the chalk lines marked in Step 2, plumb the jamb from side to side with a carpenter's level *(left)*, and nail the plate to the floor with $2\frac{1}{2}$-inch common nails.

◆ Repeat the procedure with the split stud.

◆ At the top of the split jamb, nail through the predrilled holes in the jamb flanges into the edges of the nailing strips for each track *(inset)*.

## 5. Hanging the door.

◆ Draw a center line along the top edge of the door and, following the manufacturer's spacing instructions, use a wrench to drive the four hex-head screws provided with the unit to within $\frac{1}{4}$ inch of the surface *(inset)*.

◆ Turn the adjuster on one of the gliders to extend the slotted bracket and fit the glider wheel into the part of the track that runs into the door pocket.

◆ With a helper, hold the door partway inside the pocket, push the slots of the glider bracket under one pair of screws *(right)* and tighten them.

◆ Slide the door farther into the pocket and install the second glider in the same way but facing the opposite direction and set the wheel in the part of the track that runs across the doorway.

◆ Plumb the door and raise the bottom about $\frac{1}{2}$ inch above the floor by turning the adjuster.

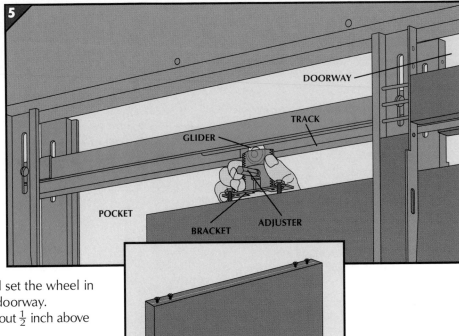

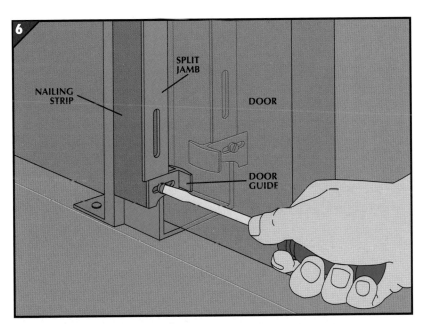

## 6. Mounting the hardware to hold the door in line.

◆ Set the slotted section of each door guide against the edge of the wooden nailing strip at the bottom of the split jamb, and drive the screw provided by the manufacturer through the slot and partially into the strip. Position each guide to leave a $\frac{1}{8}$-inch gap between the guide and the door; tighten the screw.

◆ With the screw provided by the manufacturer, fasten the rubber bumper included in the kit to the pocket jack stud, about halfway between the track and the floor.

◆ Slide the door against the bumper. The outer edge of the door should extend $\frac{3}{8}$ inch into the doorway; if it does not, either shim the bumper with a metal washer or trim it with a utility knife.

◆ Install wallboard above the opening and over the pocket, using the rough frame, the track nailing strips, and the wooden strips on the split jamb and split stud as nailing surfaces.

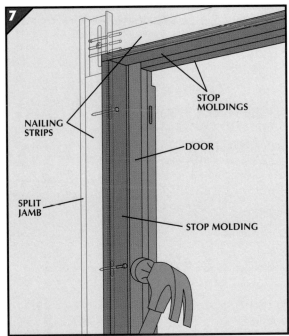

## 7. Installing stop, jamb, and casing.

◆ Along the top of the doorway, nail standard doorstop moldings to the bottom of the track nailing strips, covering the edges of the wallboard above the door and extending to within $\frac{1}{8}$ inch of it.

◆ On both sides of the pocket opening (where the door enters the pocket) nail stop moldings through the slots in the split jambs into the jamb nailing strips *(above)*.

◆ At the other side of the rough frame, fasten jamb stock to the jack stud.

◆ Install casing *(pages 29-32)* overhead and at the sides of the doorway.

**A** prehung door provides an easy way to fill a door opening, but some situations call for hanging your own door. The space available for an opening may not match any prehung door, for example, or the door you have chosen may not be available prehung.

**Hanging a New Door:** To install a new door in an existing frame, check that the new door will fit the old opening. You should be able to find one of matching thickness, but you may have to settle for a door that is slightly oversize in height and width, and then trim it to fit. You can take as much as an inch off the height of a panel or hollow-core door, and as much as 2 inches off the width; trim the width equally from both sides, but cut the height from the bottom alone. If you must saw off more than an inch from the bottom, order a solid-core door—called a flush door—which can be cut back a larger amount on any side.

**Building a Finish Frame:** To fashion a new door frame, order jamb stock that is $4\frac{5}{8}$ inches wide for standard 2-by-4 stud walls covered with wallboard or $5\frac{3}{8}$ inches wide for walls that are covered with plaster. For walls of different thicknesses, have the lumberyard mill pieces of jamb stock to the width you need or plane the stock to size.

Two grades of jamb stock are generally available. The more costly "clear" stock, made from select lumber, can be finished with stain or varnish; finger-joint stock, consisting of a number of short pieces of wood glued together, must be covered with paint. Assembling the jambs involves joint techniques like those required for windows *(page 89)*.

Order hinges, locks, and thresholds when you buy the door and the jamb stock. A solid-core door or any door taller than 6 feet 8 inches requires three hinges. For exterior and interior doors, buy locks that adjust to fit the door thickness. If you will install a dead-bolt lock in addition to the knob lock, be sure that the backset—the distance between the center of each lock and the edge of the door—is the same for both so the locks line up vertically on the face of the door. Finish up the installation by installing casing *(pages 29-32)*.

---

 **TOOLS**

Combination
  square
Carpenter's level
Metal straightedge
Plywood
  straightedge

Compass
Marking gauge
Utility knife
Awl
Mallet
Screwdriver
Wood chisel
Jack plane

Circular saw
Plywood
  edge guide
Electric drill
Countersink
  bit
Hole saw
Spade bit

 **MATERIALS**

1x2s
Stop molding
Jamb stock
Threshold
Shims
Common nails ($2\frac{1}{2}$")

Galvanized
  finishing nails
  ($1\frac{1}{2}$", $3\frac{1}{2}$")
Galvanized
  wood screws
  ($1\frac{1}{2}$" No. 8)
Hinges

 **SAFETY TIPS**

*Wear goggles to protect your eyes when hammering and operating a power saw.*

## MAKING THE SIDE JAMBS

**1. Locating dadoes in the jambs.**
◆ To the height of the door, add $\frac{5}{8}$ inch plus the thickness of carpeting or threshold. Mark this distance—representing the bottom of the head-jamb dado—on a length of jamb stock.
◆ Mark the top of the dado so the space betwen the marks equals the thickness of the jamb stock, then extend both marks across the board.
◆ Repeat the process on a second length of jamb stock and trim both pieces 1 inch above the top of the dado.

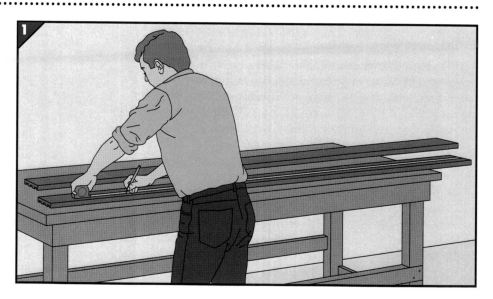

## 2. Cutting the dadoes.

◆ Clamp each of the pieces to the top of a workbench. Set a marking gauge to half the thickness of the stock and mark the depth of the dado on both edges of the jamb stock *(right)*.

◆ Cut out the dadoes as shown on pages 91-92.

JAMB STOCK

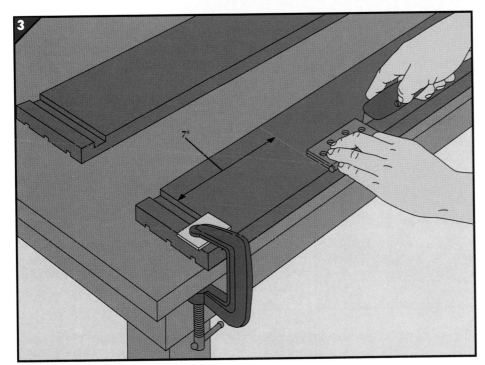

7"

## 3. Locating the hinges.

◆ On one of the side jambs make one mark 7 inches below the bottom of the dado and another 11 inches above the bottom of the jamb; extend both marks across the width of the jamb.

◆ Set a hinge, pin-side out, against each marked line: the top of the upper hinge against the top line and the bottom of the lower hinge against the other line. Score along the top and bottom of each hinge with a utility knife *(left)*.

If the door requires three hinges, locate the bottom one 7 inches above the bottom of the jamb and center the marks for the third hinge between those for the top and bottom hinges.

## 4. Marking the depth of the mortises.

◆ Set the marking gauge to the thickness of a hinge leaf *(right)*.

◆ Run the gauge along the edge of the jamb between the lines scored for each hinge.

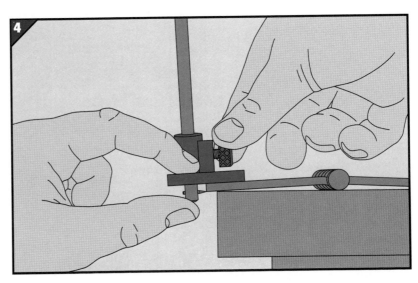

111

## 5. Completing the mortise marks.

◆ Set the marking gauge to the thickness of the door minus $\frac{3}{16}$ inch and connect the scored hinge lines on the face of the jamb. This will ensure that the hinge extends onto the jamb the same distance as onto the door *(page 117, Step 2)*.

◆ With a utility knife and a straightedge, deeply score all the hinge lines on the face and edge of the jamb.

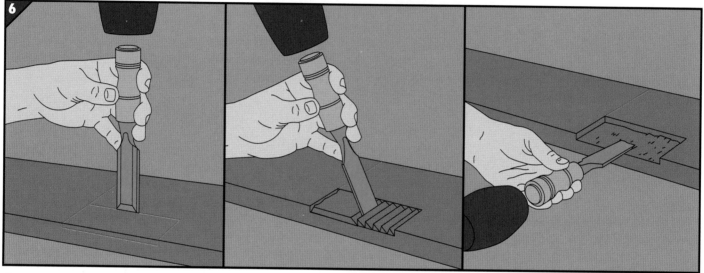

## 6. Chiseling out the mortises.

◆ With a mallet, drive a $1\frac{1}{4}$-inch chisel, held vertically with the beveled edge inward, along the scored marks on the face of the jamb *(above, left)*.

◆ Make a series of cuts, tilting the chisel slightly *(above, center)*.

◆ Work from the opposite direction to remove the chiseled wedges.

◆ Place the flat edge of the chisel against the depth mark and clean out the bottom of the mortise *(above, right)*.

A router can be paired with a simple shop-built jig *(page 117)* to cut hinge mortises. If you use a router, you will either have to square off the corners of the mortises with a chisel, or buy hinges with rounded corners.

### TRICKS OF THE TRADE

### A Hinge-Mortising Jig

This jig enables you to cut mortises with a router and a straight bit quickly and accurately. Buy a template guide for your router and install it on the base plate. Cut the jig's template from a piece of $\frac{3}{4}$-inch plywood wide enough to support the router. Outline the hinge leaf on the template, then enlarge this area to compensate for the guide and the thickness of the $\frac{3}{4}$-inch fence. Cut out this area and attach the template to the fence with countersunk screws. To make the cuts, clamp the template to the jamb stock as shown (or to the edge of a door), aligning the cutout with the outline of the hinge. Cut the mortise moving the router in small clockwise circles. Remove the jig and square the corners with a chisel. (Round-corner hinges will save you this last step.)

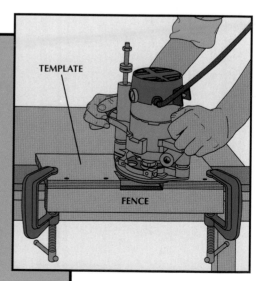

TEMPLATE

FENCE

# ASSEMBLING THE FINISH FRAME

## 1. Assembling the frame.
◆ Cut the head jamb to the width of the door plus the total depth of the dadoes and $\frac{1}{4}$ inch for clearance.
◆ Place a side jamb in a vise, sandwiched between strips of cardboard to protect it. On the outside of the jamb, use a combination square to draw a line corresponding to the center of the dado. Repeat for the other side jamb.
◆ Insert the head jamb into the dado. Drill a countersunk pilot hole and drive two $1\frac{1}{2}$-inch galvanized No. 8 wood screws along the line into the head jamb. Fasten the other side jamb to the head jamb the same way.

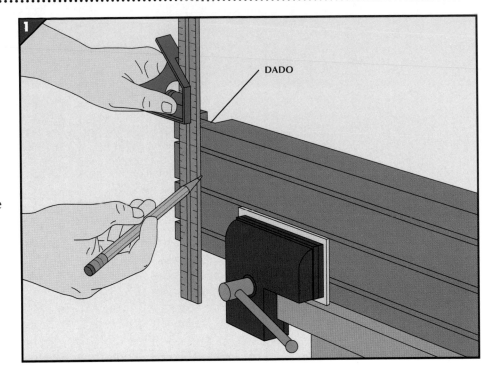

DADO

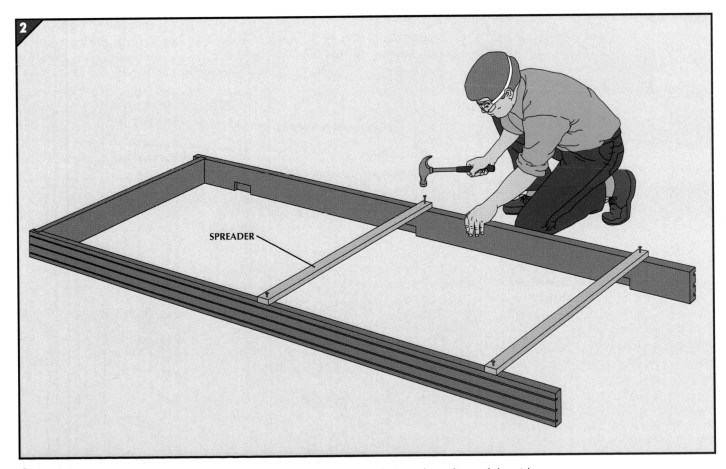

SPREADER

## 2. Bracing the frame.
◆ Cut two 1-by-2 spreaders to a length equal to the width of the assembled frame.

◆ Tack the spreaders to the edges of the side jambs with $2\frac{1}{2}$-inch common nails just below the center and bottom hinge mortises.

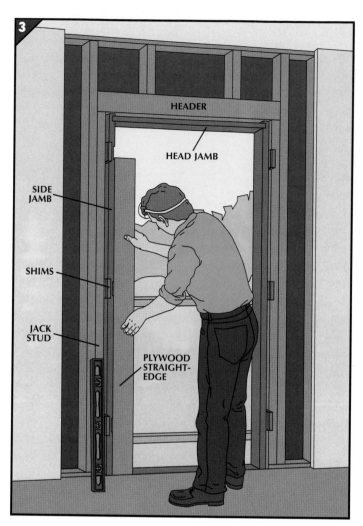

### 3. Installing the frame.

◆ Center the frame in the rough opening.

◆ Push pairs of shims between the side jambs and the jack studs at the level of the hinge mortises.

◆ With a level and the factory-cut edge of a 6-foot length of $\frac{3}{4}$-inch plywood, make sure that the hinge-side jamb is plumb and straight *(left)*, adjusting the shims to eliminate warps or bows.

◆ Shim in one place between the head jamb and the header, making sure the head jamb is straight and level.

◆ Adjust the shims on the lock side to plumb and straighten the jamb.

◆ Fasten the finish frame to the rough framing by driving two $3\frac{1}{2}$-inch galvanized finishing nails through the jambs at each pair of shims.

In the illustration, labels read: HEADER, HEAD JAMB, SIDE JAMB, SHIMS, JACK STUD, PLYWOOD STRAIGHT-EDGE.

# FITTING A DOOR TO A FRAME

### 1. Marking the height.

If you have built a new frame, sized to fit your door, go to Step 4. Otherwise:

◆ Measure the distance from the floor to the bottom of the head jamb and subtract $\frac{3}{8}$ inch plus clearance for a rug or threshold; mark this distance from the top of the door.

◆ With a combination square or a marking gauge, extend the mark across the width of the bottom of the door.

If the door has a plywood-veneer face, score the line deeply with a utility knife and metal straightedge, then score a matching line on the other side of the door.

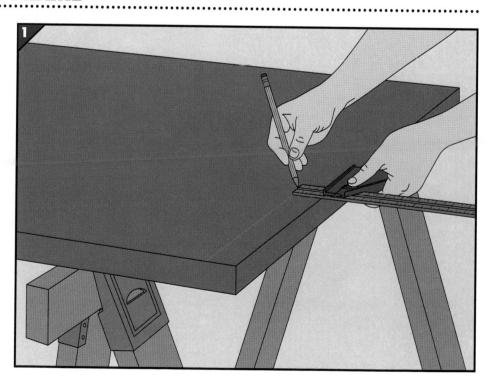

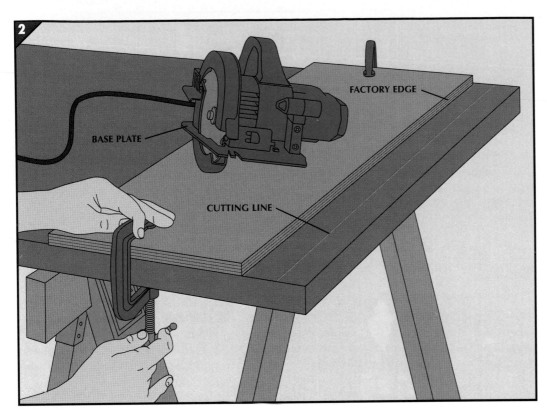

## 2. Cutting the door to length.

◆ Measure the distance between the blade of your circular saw and the edge of the saw's base plate. Clamp the straight, factory-cut edge of a piece of plywood this distance above the line you marked in Step 1 *(left)*.
◆ Set the blade $\frac{1}{8}$ inch deeper than the door thickness and saw along the plywood guide.

## 3. Sizing for width.

◆ To create $\frac{1}{8}$ inch of clearance on each side of the door, set the hinge-edge of the door against the corresponding side jamb. While a helper holds the door against the edge of the lock-side jamb, scribe the door's lock-side face by running a compass set to $\frac{1}{4}$ inch along the jamb *(right)*.
◆ Trim the door to the line with a jack plane. If you have more than about $\frac{1}{8}$ inch to remove, make a cut with a circular saw and then finish the work with a plane. If you have more than 1 inch to take off, split the amount between the two sides of the door.
◆ Attach stop molding to the head and side jambs with $1\frac{1}{2}$-inch galvanized nails *(pages 32-33, Steps 1-3)*, positioning them to allow for the thickness of the door plus a clearance of $\frac{1}{16}$ inch.

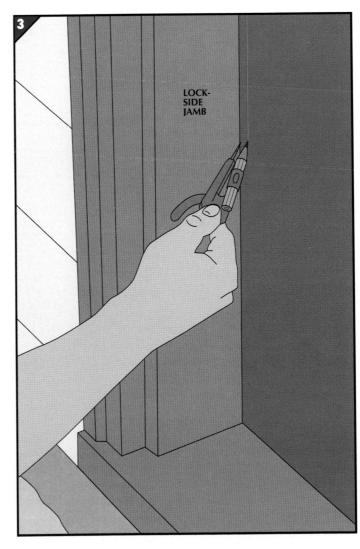

## 4. Marking a bevel.

◆ Set the spur of a marking gauge to $\frac{1}{8}$ inch.

◆ On the face of the door that will meet the doorstop, run the marking gauge along the lock-side edge *(right)*.

◆ With a ruler, draw lines across the top and bottom edges of the door to the adjacent corners.

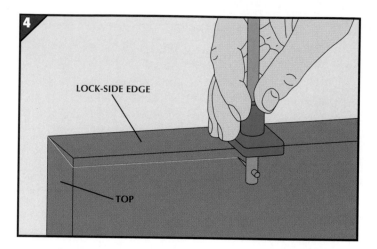

LOCK-SIDE EDGE

TOP

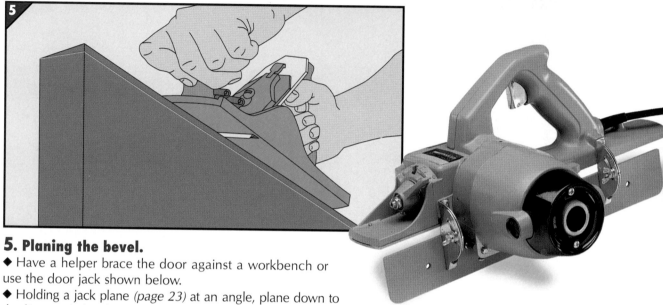

## 5. Planing the bevel.

◆ Have a helper brace the door against a workbench or use the door jack shown below.

◆ Holding a jack plane *(page 23)* at an angle, plane down to the line made by the marking gauge *(above)*. Alternatively, a portable power planer *(photograph)*, which can be set to the desired bevel angle, is handy for this job.

**TRICKS OF THE TRADE**

### A Simple Device to Hold a Door

Assembled from a few scraps of wood, a door jack offers a handy way to hold a door on edge while planing it to size or cutting hinge mortises. It is fashioned from three 1-by-2s and two 2-by-6s.

The 2-by-6s, separated by a gap $\frac{3}{8}$ inch wider than the thickness of the door, are nailed on edge to a 1-by-2 about 3 feet long. Glue cardboard strips to the inside edge of the 2-by-6s to protect the door while you work on it. Nail a pair of 1-by-2s across the bottom of the assembly to stabilize the jack and raise it above the floor. When the door is set into the jack, the weight forces the middle of the 1-by-2 down, and the 2-by-6s squeeze together to hold the door securely in place.

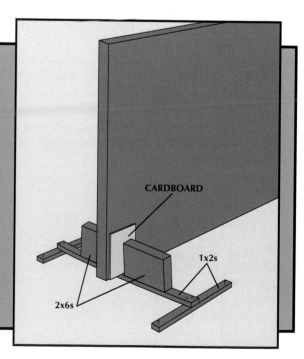

CARDBOARD

1x2s

2x6s

# PUTTING ON THE HINGES

## 1. Determining the hinge locations.

◆ With the door in the finish frame, have a helper hold two $1\frac{1}{2}$-inch nails as spacers between the top of the door and the head jamb while you drive shims beneath the door to wedge it tight against the nails.

◆ Drive a shim between the door and the lock-side jamb about 3 feet from the floor, to push the door against the hinge-side jamb.

◆ Nick the edge of the door with a utility knife at the top and bottom of each hinge mortise in the jamb *(right)*.

If you are installing the door in an old frame that may have sagged, the clearance at the head jamb may not be even. Set the arms of a compass at the widest point of the gap, scribe the top of the door, and plane the door to the scribed line.

HINGE-SIDE JAMB

LOCK-SIDE JAMB

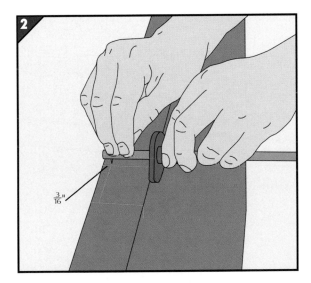

$\frac{3}{16}$"

## 2. Mortising the hinge and hanging the door.

◆ Take the door out of the frame and extend the scored lines across the hinge-side edge.

◆ Set a marking gauge to $\frac{3}{16}$ inch less than the thickness of the door. Run the gauge between each pair of hinge marks to outline the mortise to be cut, holding the gauge so the $\frac{3}{16}$-inch strip that will be left uncut is on the side abutting the doorstop *(left)*.

◆ Chisel out the hinge mortises in the door *(page 112, Step 6)*.

◆ Separate the hinge leaves by pulling out the hinge pins. Screw the leaves to the door and the jamb, making sure they are right side up.

◆ Set the door upright beside the hinge-side jamb and slip a pair of shims between the floor and the lock-side corner of the door.

◆ Join the top hinge leaves and insert the hinge pin; then repeat for the lower hinge. If the hinge leaves do not mesh, loosen the screws slightly and tap the leaves into alignment.

### A HANDY TOOL TO MARK HINGE LOCATIONS

A butt gauge will mark the hinge location with a tap of a hammer. Choose one that is the same size as the hinge you are installing. Rest the stops against the door and line up the cutting edge with a mark indicating one end of the hinge. Strike the gauge to drive the cutting edges the desired depth into the wood. Some models have a pin for marking the depth of the mortise, corresponding to the thickness of a standard hinge leaf for the depth. This eliminates the need for a marking gauge.

# CUTTING HOLES FOR A LOCK

## 1. Aligning the holes.

◆ Mark the lock-side edge of the door 36 inches above the floor and draw a line from this point across the edge and 3 inches of the door that faces away from the stop.

◆ Fold the manufacturer's template supplied with your lock over the edge and face of the door, centered on the line you made in Step 1. With a sharp pencil or an awl, pierce the paper to indicate the center of the doorknob hole on the face of the door *(right)* and the center of the latch-bolt hole on the edge.

◆ Shut the door and drill the knob hole with a hole saw; when the hole saw's guide bit breaks through the door, stop drilling and complete the hole from the other side.

◆ Drive shims beneath the door to hold it open. Equip your drill with a spade bit, then bore the latch-bolt hole through the edge of the door to meet the knob hole; take care to drill as straight as possible.

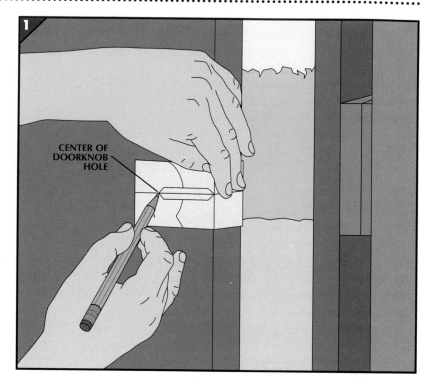

CENTER OF DOORKNOB HOLE

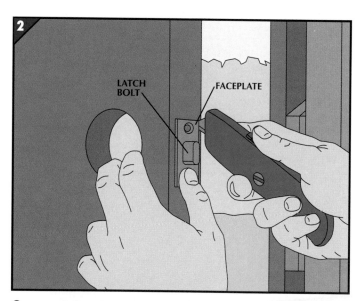

LATCH BOLT

FACEPLATE

## 2. Mortising for the latch bolt.

◆ Insert the barrel of the latch bolt in its hole, with the beveled edge of the bolt facing the doorstop, and outline the faceplate on the edge of the door with a utility knife.

◆ Chisel out a mortise as deep as the thickness of the faceplate *(page 112, Step 6)*.

◆ Screw the latch-bolt plate to the door.

### A DOOR LOCK INSTALLATION KIT

If you don't already have the tools necessary to drill holes for a new lock, consider purchasing an installation kit. It includes a sharp pin to mark the center of the holes on the door; a drill guide that fits on the edge of the door to hold your drill straight for a pilot hole to start the hole saw and spade bit; a hole to bore the hole in the face of the door; and a spade bit to drill the hole in the edge of the door.

DRILL GUIDE

HOLE SAW

SHARP PIN

SPADE BIT

### 3. Locating the strike plate.

◆ Measure from the face of the door nearest the stop to the flat side of the latch bolt with a combination square *(inset)*; measure the same distance on the jamb from the doorstop and mark a vertical line on the face of the jamb about 3 feet from the floor.

◆ Shut the door and transfer the 36-inch mark made in Step 1 to the jamb.

◆ Hold the strike plate face down against the jamb centered on the 36-inch line. Align the edges of the plate's screw holes with the vertical line *(left)* then mark the inside of the hole and the outside of the plate.

◆ With a spade bit, drill $\frac{1}{2}$ inch deep through the marked hole for the latch bolt.

◆ Chisel a mortise for the strike plate *(page 112, Step 6)* and screw the plate to the jamb.

◆ Install the lock *(pages 102-103)*.

---

**TRICKS OF THE TRADE**

### Marking the Jamb for a Deadbolt

One way to mark the location of the strike plate for a deadbolt is to coat the end of the bolt with lipstick or a grease pencil. Close the door and turn the bolt against the jamb to leave a mark. Then chisel out the mortise as explained in Step 3 *(above)*.

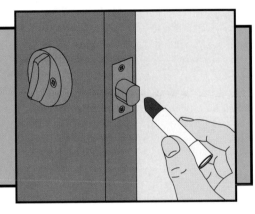

---

# A PAIR OF CAFÉ DOORS

### Installing gravity hinges.

Café doors are generally set about 12 inches above the floor, with gravity-pivot hinges at the top and bottom of each door. Each hinge consists of a jamb socket screwed to a side jamb and a pivot mounted on the top or bottom of the door; notches in the bottom hinge *(inset)* fit together to hold the door open.

◆ Mount the bottom jamb sockets on the side jambs.

◆ Screw the pivots to the top and bottom of the doors.

◆ Slip the doors into the bottom sockets.

◆ Fit the top jamb sockets over the top pivots and screw the sockets to the jambs.

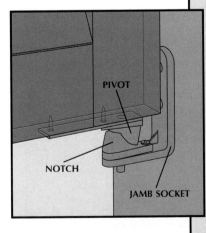

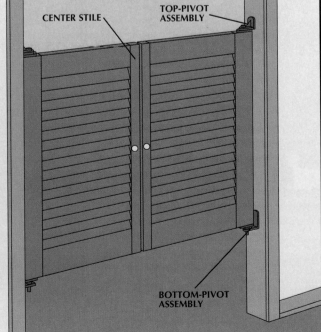

If the jambs are not plumb, plane the doors to fit—but only on the hinge sides. Otherwise, the doors will look lopsided because the center stile will not be rectangular.

# Installing a Garage Door Opener

**A**dding an automatic garage door opener to your home is not only a convenience, but also a safety feature. Most models have lights that turn on automatically, when the door is activated. There are three varieties of openers: chain-, screw-, and belt-driven. Shown here is the belt-type; the other types are installed similarly.

**Preliminary Steps:** Before installing your garage door opener, remove any ropes connected to the garage door. Disengage any existing garage door locks to avoid damaging the door. Make sure there is an outlet within reach of the power unit's cord, usually 3 to 6 feet. Do not use an extension cord.

For the opener to operate safely, the bottom of the door must meet the floor all the way across. If it does not, repair the door or floor. Also make sure the door stays in place when it is opened half way. If the springs aren't holding the door, call a professional; the springs are under great tension and can cause serious injury.

**Reinforcing the Garage Door:** On a door made of solid wood, the opener assembly is attached directly to the door. On any other type of door—fiberglass, aluminum, steel, or doors with glass panels—add metal reinforcements to the top and center, as shown below.

 **TOOLS**

| | |
|---|---|
| Screwdriver | Wire strippers |
| Wrenches | Electric drill |
| Tin snips | |

 **MATERIALS**

2x4s
Lag screws
($\frac{5}{16}$"x 2", $\frac{5}{16}$"x 3")
and washers
Bolts ($\frac{5}{16}$"), washers, and nuts

Metal support bracket
Perforated metal strapping
Angle iron

**SAFETY TIPS**

*Protect your eyes with goggles when drilling overhead.*

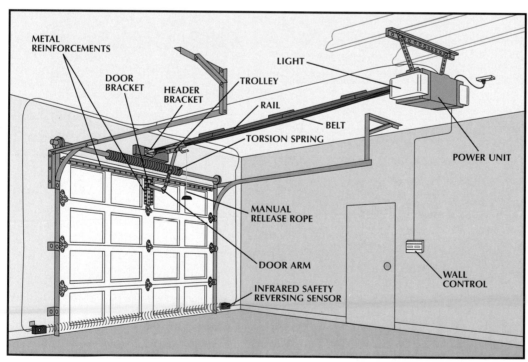

Labels: METAL REINFORCEMENTS, DOOR BRACKET, HEADER BRACKET, LIGHT, TROLLEY, RAIL, BELT, TORSION SPRING, MANUAL RELEASE ROPE, DOOR ARM, INFRARED SAFETY REVERSING SENSOR, POWER UNIT, WALL CONTROL

## Safety Checklist

✔ Do not allow children to play near the garage door or to operate controls.

✔ Never enter or leave the garage when the door is in motion.

✔ Only operate the opener when the door is in full view.

✔ Locate the garage door control out of the reach of children. Make sure the opener is in sight of the door and that it is clear of the working parts of the door.

## A garage door opener.

The garage door is operated either by a single torsion spring as shown here or by extension springs on each side of the door. When the garage door opener is activated, the trolley, attached to a belt driven by the power unit, moves away from the door along the rail. The door arm, which connects the trolley to the door, guides the door upward. When the door is closing, safety sensors located on the wall or floor near the bottom of the door automatically reverse the motion if the infrared beam between them is interrupted. The sensors can be installed on the floor instead of on the wall; consult your owner's manual. A wall control opens the door from inside the garage, and a release handle disengages the trolley allowing you to open the door manually if necessary. Metal reinforcements aren't needed for a solid wood door like this one, but they have been included to show their placement.

# ASSEMBLING THE UNIT

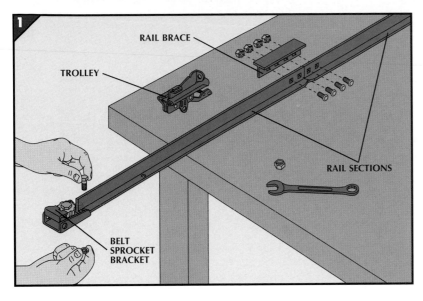

RAIL BRACE

TROLLEY

RAIL SECTIONS

BELT SPROCKET BRACKET

## 1. Putting together the rail.

◆ Line up the sections of the rail on a flat surface. Attach a rail brace at each joint with the bolts and lock nuts provided. In this model, the nuts must be on the same side of the rail as the braces to avoid obstructing the trolley.

◆ Attach the belt sprocket bracket to the front end of the rail *(left)*, keeping the bracket in line with the rail.

◆ Set a screwdriver in the hole near the front end of the rail and slide the trolley onto the rail and along it as far as the screwdriver.

◆ Fasten the rail to the top of the power unit with the screws and washers provided.

## 2. Installing the belt.

◆ Set the trolley clip into the slot on top of the trolley and feed one end of the belt around the sprocket.

◆ Attach the end of the belt to the trolley clip *(right)* by pushing the master link through the holes in the trolley clip and belt clip connector. Close the link with the cap and clip.

◆ With the trolley against the screwdriver, wrap the belt around the drive sprocket on the power unit.

◆ Fasten the end of the belt to the threaded shaft with the second master link.

◆ Push the threaded shaft through the hole in the trolley. Holding the belt, hand-tighten the spring assembly on the shaft. Remove the screwdriver.

If your opener is driven by a chain instead of a belt, follow the instructions in your owner's manual to install the chain.

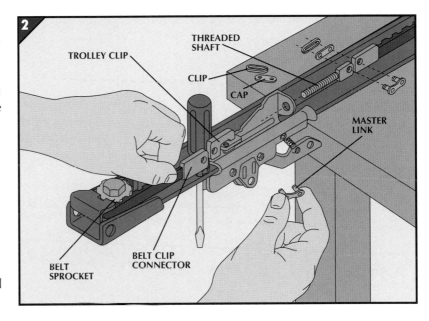

THREADED SHAFT

TROLLEY CLIP

CLIP

CAP

MASTER LINK

BELT SPROCKET

BELT CLIP CONNECTOR

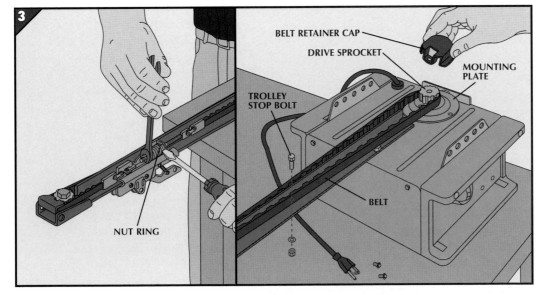

BELT RETAINER CAP

DRIVE SPROCKET

MOUNTING PLATE

TROLLEY STOP BOLT

BELT

NUT RING

## 3. Setting belt tension.

◆ Hold the nut ring in place with the tip of a screwdriver and turn the spring nut clockwise until the spring snaps open *(far left)*.

◆ Snap the retainer cap over the sprocket *(left)*, lining up the holes in the cap with the ones in the mounting plate. Fasten the cap with the screws provided.

◆ Install the trolley stop bolt in the hole in the track to prevent the trolley from hitting the motor unit.

# SECURING THE DOOR OPENER IN PLACE

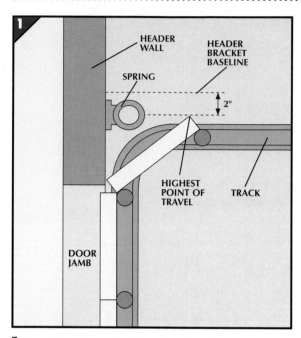

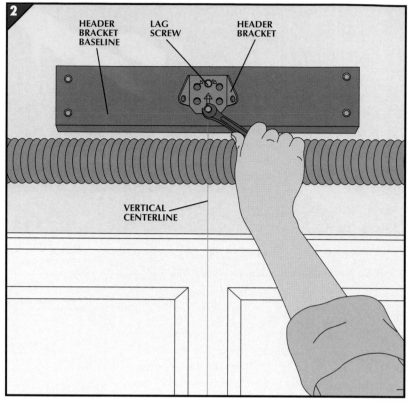

## 1. Positioning the header bracket.
◆ Open the door to find the highest point the door reaches *(above)*. Mark this point on the wall above the door.
◆ Center a 2-by-4 on the wall about 1 inch above the mark. Drill pilot holes and fasten the board to the wall header or studs with $\frac{5}{16}$-by-3-inch lag screws.
◆ Close the garage door and mark a vertical line on the center of the door and onto the 2-by-4 above the door.
◆ Measure 2 inches up from the high point of the door's path and draw a horizontal line —the header bracket baseline—intersecting the vertical centerline.

## 2. Fastening the header bracket.
◆ Align the bottom edge of the header bracket with the header bracket baseline and center it over the vertical centerline.
◆ Tack the bracket in place with a nail and mark the top and bottom holes on the 2-by-4. Remove the bracket and drill pilot holes for lag screws.
◆ Fasten the bracket with lag screws.

If there is not enough clearance above the door to attach the header bracket to the wall, it can be attached to the ceiling instead —consult your owner's manual.

## 3. Attaching the rail to the header bracket.
◆ Set the opener assembly on the floor under the header bracket and insert the belt sprocket bracket into the header bracket. You may have to angle the unit out from the door and raise it up on a box to clear the spring above the door.
◆ Align the holes in the brackets and insert a clevis pin. Secure the pin with a safety ring *(left)*.

## 4. Hanging the opener from the ceiling.

◆ Set the power unit on a stepladder.

◆ Raise the door to its fully open position.

◆ To determine the correct clearance between the door and the rail, lay a 2-by-4 flat on the top section of the door. With scraps of wood, raise or lower the unit until the rail just clears the 2-by-4 *(above, left)*.

◆ To secure the opener to a finished ceiling, fasten a metal support bracket to the joists with $\frac{5}{16}$-by-2-inch lag screws.

◆ With tin snips, cut two lengths of perforated metal strapping to fit at an angle between the power unit and the support bracket.

◆ Fasten the lengths of strapping to the opener with the bolts, lock washers, and nuts provided.

◆ Attach the other end of the strapping to the metal bracket with $\frac{5}{16}$-inch bolts *(above, right)*.

◆ For an unfinished ceiling, fasten the metal strapping directly to the joists.

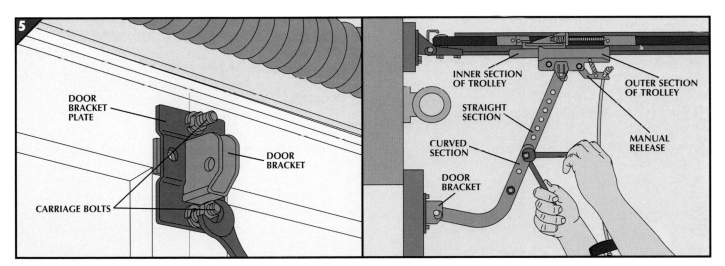

## 5. Connecting the opener to the door.

If you have a lightweight door made of fiberglass, aluminum, steel, or glass panels, reinforce it as shown in the anatomy *(page 120)* before connecting the opener. A kit containing the necessary hardware may be available from the manufacturer; if not, use lengths of angle iron.

◆ First place the door bracket at the centerline on the door, 2 to 4 inches below the top of the door. Fit the door bracket plate over the door bracket.

◆ Mark the upper and lower holes in the bracket plate on the door, then drill bolt holes through the door. (If the door has reinforcing hardware, secure the bracket directly to it.) Install the bracket with the carriage bolts provided *(above, left)*.

◆ Attach the manual release rope and handle to the trolley, knotting both ends of the rope.

◆ Close the garage door, then pull the manual release to disengage the separate outer section of the trolley. Slide this section 2 inches toward the power unit.

◆ Attach the straight section of the door arm to the trolley and the curved section to the door bracket, each with a clevis pin and safety ring.

◆ Fasten one arm section to the other with the bolts and nuts provided *(above, right)*.

# CONTROL PANEL AND SENSOR INSTALLATION

## 1. Wiring the control panel.
◆ Remove $\frac{1}{4}$ inch of insulation from one end of a two-conductor bell wire cable with wire strippers.

◆ Separate the color-coded wires and attach each wire to the appropriate screw terminal on the back of the door control *(right)*.

◆ Choose a convenient location for the control panel and attach it to the wall. Route the cable up the wall and along the ceiling to the power unit, fastening it with the insulated staples provided.

◆ Attach the wires to the appropriate terminals on the power unit *(inset)*.

◆ Plug in the power unit and install the light bulbs in the unit but do not operate the opener—the door will not close until the sensors are in place *(Step 2)*.

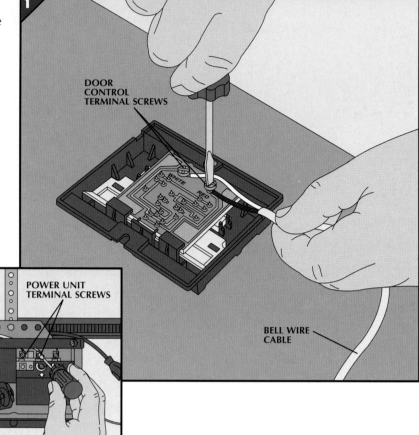

DOOR CONTROL TERMINAL SCREWS

WHITE

RED

BELL WIRE CABLE

POWER UNIT TERMINAL SCREWS

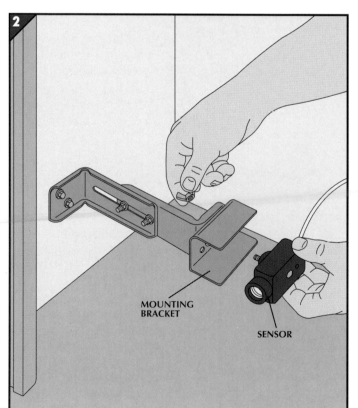

## 2. Installing the safety reverse sensors.
◆ Assemble the pieces of the mounting brackets.

◆ Position one bracket next to the door 4 to 6 inches above the floor in line with a wall stud. Mark the screw holes on the wall, remove the bracket, and drill pilot holes for the lag screws. Fasten the bracket to the wall then install the other bracket at the same height on the other side of the door.

◆ Adjust the bracket assemblies so they project the same distance from the wall.

◆ Secure the sensors to the brackets with the lenses pointing toward each other. Leave the screw on one sensor a little loose to allow for adjustments.

◆ Route the cable from each sensor up the wall and along the ceiling, fastening it with insulated staples. Connect the two wires to the power unit.

◆ Check that the sending and receiving sensors are aligned vertically and horizontally. In this model, a green light shines continuously on both sensors when they are properly aligned.

The sensors can be installed on the floor instead of on the wall if necessary—check your manual for directions.

MOUNTING BRACKET

SENSOR

## Adjusting the Limits and Force

Garage door openers are safe if properly adjusted to reverse when an obstacle is encountered. You can adjust the force with which the door opens and closes as well as the up and down limits of the door's path. After each of the following checks, make any necessary adjustments and then repeat the check. If you fail to make all of the adjustments satisfactorily, have the opener serviced by a professional.

✔ Press the wall control button to reengage the two parts of the trolley.

✔ Press the wall control button to open the door. If the door opens at least 5 feet but not completely, increase the up travel. If it opens less than 5 feet, increase the up force.

✔ Push the wall control button to close the door. If the door fails to close completely, increase the down travel. If the opener reverses when it reaches the ground, decrease the down travel. If the opener reverses while closing and the opener lights are flashing, the sensors are obstructed—remove the obstruction. If the lights are not flashing, increase the down force.

✔ While the door is opening, grasp the bottom when it is about halfway up, keeping yourself out of the path of the sensors. If the door does not stop easily, decrease the up force.

✔ Begin closing the door and grip it when it is halfway down, again staying out of the path of the sensors. If the door does not reverse easily, decrease the down force.

✔ Once the limits and force have been adjusted, be sure to conduct the safety tests described below. You can then install the light covers on the sides of the unit.

✔ Repeat the tests for the safety reversing sensors and the safety reverse system every month, and after any repairs or adjustments to the door, opener, or garage floor.

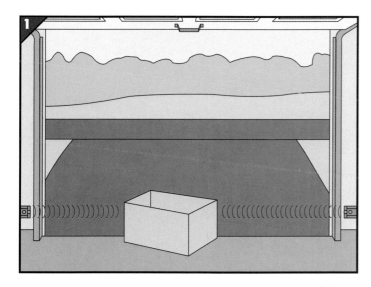

## 1. Testing the safety sensors.

If the sensor beam is obstructed, you should not be able to close the door with the remote; however, the wall button will still operate the door if it is pressed continuously.

◆ Open the door fully.

◆ Place a carton in the path of the invisible light beam between the two sensors.

◆ Press the remote button to close the door. The door should not move more than 1 inch and the sensor lights should flash. If the door does not stop immediately, check that the sensors are properly aligned (opposite, Step 2). If the door still does not reverse, call a professional.

## 2. Testing the safety reverse system.

◆ Lay a 2-by-4 board under the center of the garage door.

◆ Start closing the door. If it does not reverse when it hits the board, increase the down travel limit, and repeat the test. If you do not succeed in adjusting the door to reverse properly, call a professional.

◆ Once the door is adjusted to reverse properly, repeat the tests for the force and limits at the top of the page.

**EAU CLAIRE DISTRICT LIBRARY**

Time-Life Books is a division of Time Life Inc.

**TIME LIFE INC.**
PRESIDENT and CEO: George Artandi

**TIME-LIFE BOOKS**
PRESIDENT: John D. Hall
PUBLISHER/MANAGING EDITOR:
Neil Kagan

**HOME REPAIR AND IMPROVEMENT:**
**Windows and Doors**
EDITOR: Lee Hassig
DIRECTOR, NEW PRODUCT DEVELOP-
MENT: Quentin S. McAndrew
MARKETING DIRECTOR: James Gillespie
Text Editor: Denise Dersin
Art Director: Mary Gasperetti
Associate Editors/Research and Writing:
Tom Neven, Terrell Smith
Marketing Manager: Wells Spence
Editorial Assistant: Amy S. Crutchfield

Vice President, Director of Finance:
Christopher Hearing
Vice President, Book Production:
Marjann Caldwell
Director of Operations: Eileen Bradley
Director of Photography and Research:
John Conrad Weiser
Director of Editorial Administration:
Judith W. Shanks
Production Manager: Marlene Zack
Quality Assurance Manager: James King
Library: Louise D. Forstall

**ST. REMY MULTIMEDIA INC.**
President and Chief Executive Officer:
Fernand Lecoq
President and Chief Operating Officer:
Pierre Léveillé
Vice President, Finance: Natalie Watanabe
Managing Editor: Carolyn Jackson
Managing Art Director: Diane Denoncourt
Production Manager: Michelle Turbide

Staff for Windows and Doors

Series Editors: Pierre Home-Douglas,
Heather Mills
Series Art Director: Francine Lemieux
Art Directors: Norman Boudreault,
Jean-Pierre Bourgeois, Michel Giguère
Assistant Editor: Rebecca Smollett
Designers: François Daxhelet, Jean-Guy
Doiron, Robert Labelle, François Longpré
Editorial Assistants: Stacey Berman,
James Piecowye
Coordinator: Dominique Gagné
Copy Editor: Judy Yelon
Indexer: Christine M. Jacobs
Systems Coordinator: Éric Beaulieu
Other Staff: Marc Cassini, Joe Delaney,
Lorraine Doré, Geneviève Monette

**PICTURE CREDITS**
Cover: Photograph, Robert Chartier. Art,
Robert Paquet. Window provided by
Marvin Windows & Doors

Illustrators: Gilles Beauchemin, Michel
Blais, Roger C. Essley, Fred Holz, Joan S.
McGurren, Jacques Perrault, Jeff Swarts.

Photographers: **End papers**: Robert Chartier.
**12, 40, 50, 52, 64, 100, 117, 118**:
Robert Chartier. **30**: Sears Craftsman.
**49**: Wagner Spray Tech Corp. **69**: De-
Walt Industrial Tool Company Inc. **76**:
Keller Industries Inc. **102**: Preso-Matic
Keyless Locks. **116**: Delta International
Machinery/Porter-Cable.

**ACKNOWLEDGMENTS**
The editors wish to thank the following indi-
viduals and institutions: American Tool Cos.,
Kenosha, WI; Andersen Windows, Bayport,
MN; Appleton Supply Co. Inc., Appleton,
WI; Jon Arno, Troy, MI.; Barry Supply Co.
(Division of Barry Industries), New York, NY;
Biltbest Windows, St. Genevieve, MO;
Black & Decker Canada Inc., Richmond
Hill, Ont.; Blaine Window Hardware Inc.,
Hagerstown, MD; Bob Campbell, Preso-
Matic Keyless Locks, Sanford, FL; The
Chamberlain Group Inc., Elmhurst, IL; Delta
International Machinery/Porter-Cable, Guelph,
Ont.; DeWalt Industrial Tool Company Inc.,
Richmond Hill, Ont.; The Fletcher-Terry
Company Inc., Formington, CT; J. Dennis
Gordon Advertising and Marketing, Planta-
tion, FL; Hyde Tools, Southbridge, MA;
Joanne The Shutter Company, Charlotte,
NC; Keller Industries Inc., Fort Lauderdale,
FL; Karl Marcuse, Montreal, Que.; Marvin
Windows & Doors, Warroad, MN and Mis-
sissauga, Ont.; Mutual Materials Company,
Bellevue, WA; Quaker City Manufacturing
Co., Folcroft, PA; Sears Craftsman, Schaum-
burg, IL.; Shandwick USA, Bloomington, IL;
Stanley Door Systems, Troy, MI; Stanley
Hardware, New Britain, CT; Wagner Spray
Tech Corp., Minneapolis, MN; Weather
Shield Mfg., Inc., Medford, WI; Woodcraft
Supply Co., Parkersburg, WV

**Library of Congress**
**Cataloging-in-Publication Data**
Windows and doors / by the editors of
Time-Life Books.
p. cm. — (Home repair and improve-
ment)
Includes index.
ISBN 0-7835-3902-9
1. Windows—Maintenance and repair—
Amateurs' manuals. 2. Doors—Mainte-
nance and repair—Amateurs' manuals.
I. Time-Life Books. II. Series.
TH2270.W63 1996
690'.1823—dc20                96-15726